glass
fibre
yachts

glass
fibre
yachts
improvement
and repair
Charles Jones

illustrated by Peter A. G. Milne

 Nautical

First published in Great Britain by
NAUTICAL PUBLISHING COMPANY
Lymington, Hampshire, SO4 9BA

First published 1972
Reprinted 1974
ISBN 0 245 50801 5

Filmset and printed in Great Britain by
BAS Printers Limited, Wallop, Hampshire.

CONTENTS

8 Cockpit locker racks

8 Binocular bo

9 Book cas

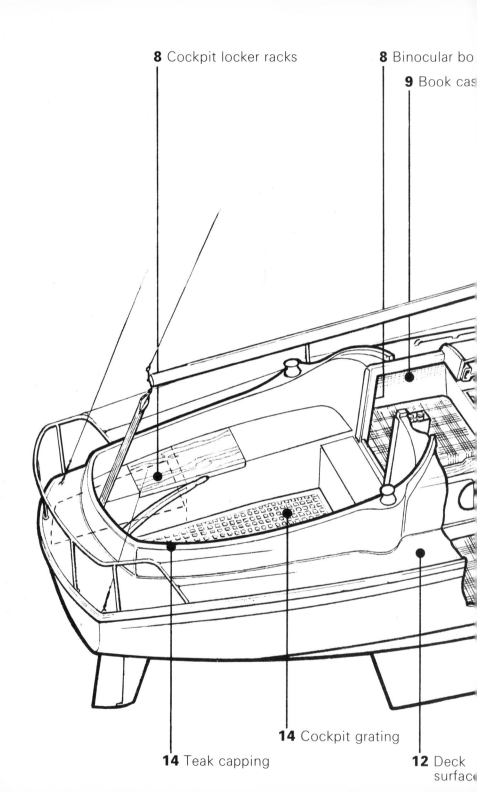

14 Cockpit grating

14 Teak capping

12 Deck
surface

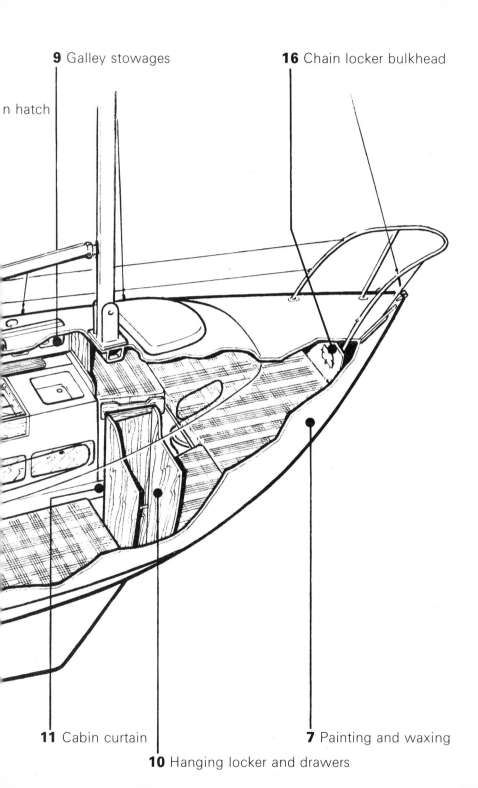

9 Galley stowages

16 Chain locker bulkhead

n hatch

11 Cabin curtain

10 Hanging locker and drawers

7 Painting and waxing

by the same author

How now, Brown cow
Germans under my bed
Head in the Sand
People in Boats
Around Llangollen
Around Helston and the Lizard
Come Cruising (co-author)
More fun from your boat
Maintenance for boat owners

1 The materials, and how they came to a common application. The first G.R.P. boats. Design and construction. The principles of improvement.

Glass fibre, fibre glass, G.R.P., plastic, a blessing, an abomination. Whatever the nomenclature and the personal point of view, when the yachtsman refers to it he is speaking of the material from which about seventy-five per cent of all pleasure craft—sail and motor—are built in Britain today.

The proportion is about the same in France, higher in Italy, lower in Spain. In the United States there are sometimes indications that the level is falling from its high point of about eighty per cent; sometimes the proportion seems to be creeping up. But it is obvious that it has come to stay as a boat building material in a world civilization which is crowding itself off the land and on to the water.

How many people know what it is, how a boat is built from it, and why spun glass and resin should even have been brought together as a composite material in the first place? Before we can get down to a discussion of methods of improving a glass fibre yacht, it is essential to have some understanding of the material and the methods of building with it.

Synthetic resins have been available for many years. They were not difficult to produce; but in the beginning there seemed to be very little application for them. On their own, they are brittle materials; and they achieved little success in the favourite pre-war field for plastics—buttons, photo frames and egg cups. No doubt some use was made of them in industry, but the yearly tonnage produced was very small.

The fact that molten glass can be pulled into very fine threads has also been known for a very long time—ever since man first burned his fingers prodding the stuff, no doubt. Here again, it was a knowledge which seemed to have very little application. The Victorians made elaborate ornaments of spun glass, but what else could be done with it? The fact that, if drawn fine enough through a nozzle, glass was nearly as flexible as silk seemed to have little application, though a garment of woven glass was made for a princess in the middle of last century. By all reports, it was not successful.

Various materials were used to reinforce synthetic resins in the 1930s, but tensile strength achieved was very poor. Then, in the

Second World War, came the rapid development of radar, and it was discovered early on that the all-important reflective surface of the scanner should have a cover. This was both to disguise it from the enemy and to protect it from deterioration. A cover, however, had to be made of a material which would not affect either the power or the path of the radar pulses, yet be strong, and resistant to weather.

No doubt a number of possible materials came under review. At some point in the proceedings, scientists tried reinforcing synthetic resin with glass fibres; and discovered that the two materials, too brittle to be of much use on their own, combined to form not only a product which allowed radar pulses to pass without interruption, but had a surprising amount of tensile strength and impact resistance. It was, moreover, rust and rot proof.

After the war there was no difficulty in finding a thousand and one uses for glass fibre laminates, replacing metal and wood; for G.R.P., as it soon came to be known, appeared to be almost indestructible. In the beginning, of course, it was a very expensive material, the reinforcement being very fine glass spun and woven into cloth. But it was not long before the experimenters discovered that much coarser glass fibres could be used without detracting from the strength of the finished laminate, and costs started to fall.

The First Boats

G.R.P. boats were first moulded in America in 1945, where they came in for a great deal of derision. The laughter sounded very similar to that accorded to the first iron ship builders more than a century before. Everyone knew that iron/G.R.P. would not float. . . .

Of course, the early builders in glass reinforced plastics had no parameters, and no guides as to the actual tensile strength of the material. They therefore over-played on the side of caution, and the craft they produced were heavy and clumsy for their size; a fact which increased the hilarity of yachtsmen and conventional boatbuilders. However, possible advantages in the material were seen in one or two important quarters, and the U.S. Coastguard was quick off the mark in ordering several craft for experimental purposes. That organization works its boats hard; and every year a panel was cut from the side of a boat and examined for fatigue, weathering and other deterioration. According to reports, they found no significant changes over a ten year period.

In the meantime, more was being learned about the properties of synthetic resins reinforced with glass fibre. It was discovered, for instance, that it was not necessary to use expensively woven cloth; ample strength was obtained by the use of random chopped strand mat, a material made by chopping the glass into short fibres, two or three inches long, and allowing them to fall together in random directions to make a felt-like material. It was discovered, too, that a hull of G.R.P. could be made thinner than wood for an equal strength; that it did not need nearly so much reinforcement in the way of frames as did a timber hull; and that if it was damaged, it was much easier to repair than wood.

All this came slowly and very much empirically. Lloyd's of London later worked out some standards to which glass fibre boats should be built, and offered their valuable seal of approval if these standards were followed. But even ten years ago I remember talking to a designer who had asked Lloyd's to help him with the scantlings for a large G.R.P. sailing yacht. He was complaining bitterly that Lloyd's did not know what they were talking about—if he were to put in the weight of material they recommended the yacht, he said, would sink straight to the bottom!

While difficulties were being sorted out, boat builders who were accustomed to getting only two or three yachts a year off their slips, started to realize that the material offered, for the first time, a means of quantity production. Many of them tried it, in a tentative manner. In doing so they helped to stimulate a demand for boats, which was, in any case, already showing signs of phenomenal increase. Building a glass fibre hull is not a difficult nor a particularly expensive job. It can be 'laid-up' in a fraction of the time it takes to build a similar one in wood. But the preparation before production starts is expensive, and this is something which cannot be skimped.

Building in G.R.P.

First of all, it is necessary that a boat be designed especially for G.R.P. construction; its requirements are quite different from those of other materials. If an old-established class dinghy, for example one which has always been built of wood, is now required in glass fibre, then a set of new scantlings must be worked out. It may be possible to work within the class weight, but some sacrifices must probably be made; for example, it may be necessary to mould a foredeck thinner than is wise, this being accepted by the Class in view of the other benefits brought by the material.

The standard method of building in G.R.P. is as follows; first of all a model of the outside skin of the hull is constructed to its exact dimensions. Known as the 'plug', this is usually no more than lathe and plaster; but in the case, say, of a class dinghy, where a large number of moulds all exactly the same may be required over the years, the plug may be more durable and itself constructed of G.R.P.

In any case, a great deal of trouble and time is taken to get it exactly right, with a finish as smooth and perfect as possible. From this the mould or moulds will be made, and from the mould the hulls; so all imperfections in the plug will be repeated in every hull subsequently made.

Once the plug is as perfect as may be, it is coated with an oily substance known as a release agent, designed to prevent resin adhering to it. Glass fibre saturated with resin is then built up to a good thickness all round it, with heavy support timbers moulded in. When this is dry—'cured' is the technical term—this shell is lifted off the plug and turned the right way up.

This is the mould, and it is obvious that it is the inside surface of the mould, transferred from the plug, which equals the outside dimensions intended for the finished hull. The yacht will therefore be laid-up inside the mould, and its outside skin will have the perfections, or otherwise, of the inside of the mould.

Much additional work is therefore put into the mould, and a couple of men may take several weeks to get the perfect finish; sanding, polishing, filling in and smoothing off small irregularities. The timber supports bonded into the outside of the mould are to make sure that it cannot distort, and these may be further strengthened as felt necessary.

It is obvious that, by the time a design has been commissioned and completed, the plug and mould made, the G.R.P. hull has already cost a considerable sum. If only one yacht is to come from it, this cost is passed on to the buyer, and his vessel will be an expensive one. But this seldom happens; the builder will hope to sell at least ten hulls of the one design, all from the same mould, and its cost is spread over them. If he is very sanguine, his expectations may run to several hundred similar hulls, in which case the mould costs are easily written off.

Moulding a Hull

The materials used in the moulding of a hull are polyester resin, an accelerator, and a catalyst which is usually a peroxide. These are the flesh of the boat; its bones are provided by the glass fibres, which are used (a) in the form of random mat, already described, and (b) as a woven cloth. This latter is available in a variety of weaves, and is most commonly used now for a smooth inside finish to a hull. Another form in which the glass comes is as rovings, which are really glass fibre 'string' of various thicknesses. These are commonly used only in lay-up machines, in which the glass is chopped up small enough to be blown through the nozzle of a gun.

In possession of a mould and the necessary materials, the method of constructing the hull is as follows. The inside of the mould is coated with release agent, and then with a mixture of resin and pigment called the 'gel coat'. This will form the outside skin of the hull, and as the appearance of the yacht would be spoiled if glass fibre showed through it, no glass is mixed with this coat.

On top of the gel coat comes the first layer of glass. The material, cloth or random mat, is cut carefully to shape, so that it fits into the mould without bulging at the overlaps. Resin, mixed with accelerator and catalyst, is brushed liberally over this, and stippled and rolled well in so that it saturates the glass material, and all air bubbles are excluded.

More layers of glass and resin are applied until the requisite thicknesses are obtained, and the hull is left to 'cure', or harden off. This may take several days, but presently the hull can be lifted from the mould and left to stand free to finish curing, while another hull is laid up in its place.

The inside of the hull is sometimes given a final layer of woven glass cloth for added neatness, but it is obvious that the inside can never be as fair and smooth as the outside. In more expensive craft some sort of decorative lining is often used to trim the interior of the cabin wherever the G.R.P. is otherwise exposed. In cheaper boats a coat of emulsion paint is all it is likely to get.

There is rather more to moulding a hull than is indicated in the pages above—and it is extra skill and care which often makes all the difference between a good G.R.P. moulding and a bad one. To make one shell thicker than another is relatively inexpensive, and may not necessarily mean giving it added quality or strength. The salient factor in moulding G.R.P. with 'cold cure' resins is (a) correct mixture of resin with accelerator and catalyst, and (b) stringent environmental control. That is, the temperature and humidity of the workshop are extremely important.

'Cold cure' resins are actually hardened by heat, caused by the chemical reaction of the catalyst. Only comparatively small quantities of this are involved as far as we are concerned, for once the ingredients are mixed the pot life is fairly limited. In the actual laying up of a hull, a number of workmen can use a large quantity of resin in a short time, but in our amateur applications we shall in all likelihood never need to mix more than half a pint at once.

The resin we buy will, in fact, already have the accelerator mixed with it, so that is one factor we do not have to worry about. But the catalyst will be mixed in proportions something like 120 to 1, and the amount is therefore critical. Too much will generate too much heat, drying off the resin too quickly and making it brittle. Whereas if too little is used, the resin will fail to harden within a reasonable time and our work may take days to cure, if it does so at all. Temperature and humidity, though important to the moulder laying up complete hulls, cannot easily be brought into our calculations. The best we can do is do the work, as far as possible, on a warm day.

It can be seen, now, of just what a glass fibre hull consists. It is a solid mass of flexible glass strands embedded in polyester resin. Both resin and glass are extremely vulnerable on their own, but have excellent strength combined. G.R.P. has some of the properties of wood, in that it may be sawn and drilled (a saw for metal is best). It does not, however, have the resilience of wood, the quality which enables the latter to hold nails and screws.

Fastening to G.R.P.

When fastening things to a G.R.P. hull, therefore, screws and nails cannot be used—at least, not in the same way as in a wooden hull. This has led to the supposition that very little in the way of addition or alteration can be accomplished with G.R.P. yachts.

This is not true, and I shall be describing various useful methods of fastening things to glass fibre. We have to use, in place of conventional fastenings:

Bolts These should always be of stainless steel which is costly, gunmetal or some other non-corrodible metal such as Monel-metal. Bolts should always be provided with large diameter washers, and never themselves bear directly on to glass fibre.

Rawlnuts A patent fixing device obtainable in various lengths and diameters. To be used, usually in combination with other methods, in places easily accessible and not in contact with salt water.

Polyester resin and glass tape This is the material from which the hull is made, and is therefore the most obvious method of fastening. If not used correctly, however, there is danger of it providing very little strength in the join.

Glues   The only glue which can be relied upon to bond wood and other materials to G.R.P. is epoxy resin adhesive. Careful preparation of the wood is necessary, and it is expensive.

It is a question of selecting the right method, or combination of methods, for each individual job. In later chapters I describe particular jobs and the fastening methods used and these lead by natural progression to deciding on which type of fastening to employ for any other work which may be tackled.

2 Types of resin. Repair kits for small jobs. Disposal of resin waste; care with the accelerator. Buying reasonable quantities of tape and resin.

Two types of synthetic resin are commonly used in boat construction —polyester and epoxide. Epoxide is about four times as expensive as polyester, and the satisfactory curing of it is a more complicated business. It is fortunate, therefore, that when reinforced with glass fibres, polyester resin has ample strength for the moulding of boat hulls—and indeed for many other purposes.

Epoxy resins do have greater bonding powers than polyester, however, and are often used for this purpose—to bond a deck moulding to the hull, wooden superstructure to a G.R.P. deck, and so on.

The commercial moulders of hulls do, of course, buy their resin in large quantities from chemical companies who would not be pleased to receive an order for a couple of pounds. There are a number of firms, however, which specialize in providing small quantities for do-it-yourself people. Their trade is not confined to boat owners, for glass fibre is commonly used for many other purposes by the individual who makes his own garden pond, fabricates a new body for his sports car, makes a fish tank and translucent sheets for his sun lounge roof.

For the very small job it is possible to buy from any garage or marine chandlers a G.R.P. repair kit which usually contains resin, catalyst, brushes, glass mat, tape, spatula and plastic cups for mixing. The owner of a glass fibre yacht is wise always to have such a kit on board—he will never know when it is likely to come in handy. Generally speaking these kits will not contain enough of any material for the jobs we will want to do; and they are, in any case, an expensive way to buy. It is best, therefore, to go to one of the companies which, as I say, specialize in the kind of quantities we shall use—their advertisements can be found in the yachting press.

The resin we buy, by the pound, will normally include its accelerator, but it is a good idea to check that this is so. The catalyst may be supplied either as a paste in a toothpaste-type tube, or as a clear liquid, according to the supplier. It is much easier to measure exact quantities of a liquid, but the instructions with the paste will advise 'an inch of paste' with so much resin. It is important to make sure that the accelerator is included, already mixed with the resin, because many commercial firms buy the materials separately, preferring to mix their own in order to adjust the rate of cure to their own choice.

Only small quantities of resin and catalyst should be mixed at one time, chiefly in order to avoid waste. A fraction too much hardener and the resin starts to gel almost before mixing—and as soon as that happens it cannot be used. The only thing to do then is to discard the mix and make up another quantity, using less catalyst. It is important to note here that resin which has 'gone off' too quickly because too much catalyst was mixed with it, should not just be left in a corner for later disposal. A great deal of heat is generated during the 'going off' process, and more than one boatyard has been razed to the ground because someone jettisoned hardening resin carelessly. I have more than once had a cupful of resin burst into flames before my eyes. It is a good idea to keep a bucket of water handy for just such an eventuality. There should never be any reason for us to buy epoxide resin, but if required it is usually available from the same companies which sell polyester resin.

Glass reinforcement for the resin is available as chopped strand mat, which looks very much like thin felt of the cheaper kind sold for carpet underlay. We are likely to use this only if repairing a hole in the hull, or for heavy reinforcement—I used it successfully to bond a hardwood keel on to my plywood dinghy. We may also use it for moulding a bulkhead, or partition. Or the glass is supplied as various kinds of woven material—as a cloth of various weights, loose or fine weave; or as a tape of various widths.

It is the tape which will be of most use in making additions and alterations to the hull. A tape of two inches wide is best, and it should be of fairly loose weave. This not only makes complete saturation easier, but allows it to take a curve on its plane, if necessary.

As with the resin, glass fibre is bought by boatbuilders in quantity from large manufacturers. Glass tape is usually obtainable from marine chandlery shops; but again it is a good idea to go direct to the firms which specialize in supplying the small user. It is much cheaper in the long run; and much more convenient if, like me, you find one firm which supplies everything—resin, glass material, resin putty, brushes, strippers for cleaning the brushes, measurers, etc.

I find I can buy polyester and epoxy resin in 3 lb. tins; resin stripper in 2-pint cans (this must not be used to clean resin from the skin, as it is highly caustic); catalyst in paste form in 1-oz. tubes, or as a clear liquid in 2-oz. bottles; syringes for measuring up to 10 cc. of the liquid catalyst (these cost, at time of writing, only 15p., so there is no point in trying to guess quantities). I also buy Rozalex barrier cream from the same source. A barrier cream should always be used when working with resin, as the latter is otherwise extremely difficult to remove from the skin, and can set up dermatitis.

It is, too, possible to buy accelerator separately from the resin. If this is done, never make the mistake of mixing catalyst and accelerator together first—they have an explosive reaction to each other. The accelerator should be mixed into the resin and then the catalyst. From the same firm I buy my chopped strand mat in weights of 1 oz., 1½ oz., and 2 oz., per square foot. This is made in rolls of 36 in. wide, and I can buy it by the square yard in small quantities. Should I be intending to mould my own 50 ft yacht, I should buy it by the pound.

Glass fibre tape is obtainable in widths of from ½ in. to 6 in. and the 2 in. tape which I use costs (at the moment) 4p a yard, or if I buy a whole roll of 50 yards, 3p a yard. The same firm will also sell me carbon fibres, if I want them (they are expensive, but enable high tensile strength to be obtained for less weight than when using glass), woven glass fabric, and rovings.

In fact, this company, and others like it, is willing to supply me with everything I need, from respirators, mould materials, release agents, and even a two-part mixture for making my own polyurethane foam. I recommend that anyone contemplating working on his own G.R.P. boat should seek out a firm such as this (they nearly all run an efficient postal supply service, if there is not one near enough to be visited) and obtain their catalogue. It is better, of course, if you can call on them and see exactly what they do have to offer. I never come away from the headquarters of the firm I deal with in Brentford, without planning to mould a new yacht from scratch.

3 Ship's carpentry and the use of modern glues, cold setting types, acid and alkali hardeners. Which wood with which glue. Staining. Carpenters' cutting tools. Sharpening, types of cramp, and screwdrivers.

Improvements to a glass fibre hull sometimes mean subtracting from it, but more often making additions. Sometimes it may be possible to buy the item it is intended to add—a beautiful teak bookshelf of exactly the right size to hang over the skipper's bunk, for example.

In small cruising yachts, however, it is very unusual indeed to be able to buy something which fits. Nearly everything has to be made to tuck into corners which would—almost—be waste space otherwise! We think in a completely different set of dimensions from furniture makers, or even the owners of 50 ft yachts.

We have, therefore, to become our own ship's carpenter which, for the ham-handed, might be a frightening thought. However, the sort of work involved is well within the competence of most people, if only they will try their hands at it; for traditional work, particularly where joints are concerned, has not been absolutely necessary since waterproof resin glues were invented—although well-made joints are still a joy to the eye.

Modern Glues   Modern glues are so powerful that, once the glue line is properly set, the grain of the wood ought to break before the glue. Moreover, they are simple to use—no longer do we need the double glue pot bubbling over a fire of off-cuts, and the sticky, smelly brown mess which in our youth we believed to be made from horses' hooves.

What glues are there? Among the many available to the boat-builder there are three main types of use to us to a greater or lesser extent weatherproof, boil proof and fungus proof. They are:
(a)   Urea-formaldehyde adhesive.
(b)   Resorcinal and resorcinal-phenol-formaldehyde adhesives.
(c)   Epoxide resin adhesive.

These three types are available in small quantities and, more important, in forms which can be used cold. Boatbuilders often make use of heat-setting; and in fact it is not too difficult even for us to use heat for added speed and perhaps slightly better adhesion. We can arrange for a fan heater or even an oil stove, with heat-retaining blankets to direct the heat on to the joints, for example. The glue manufacturers are always willing to give advice on how to go about individual cases—though they naturally like to think the inquirer is going to use enough of their product to make it worth while.

On the whole, it is simpler to stick to the cold setting forms of these three main types. Those I have used and can vouch for are:
Urea-formaldehyde—Aerolite 306 with hardener GBP.X.
Resorcinal-phenol—Cascophen PC-1 with hardener PX 23.
Resorcinal-phenol-formaldehyde—Aerodux 500 with hardener 501.
Epoxide resin—Araldite AV 100 with hardener HV 100. Epophen and Epophen hardener.

Urea formaldehyde glues are usually two-part products, resin and formic acid. The resin may be supplied either in liquid form or as a powder to be mixed with water; this liquid is applied to one half of the joint, and the hardener, or catalyst, to the other. The two parts are then brought together and cramped in position.

Aerolite 306

Aerolite 306 is supplied in handyman packs as a white powder in a tin, the acid hardener in a bottle. The powder can be mixed with cold water, and I have always done so, although the manufacturers do say that it is better with the water warmed to around 20–35°C. All lumps must be beaten out, and the mixture should be left standing for about ten minutes to allow air bubbles to disperse.

Only sufficient water should be added to the powder to make a thick, limited-flow liquid (something like the consistency of golden syrup). Once this is applied to the wood, a few minutes should be allowed to lapse, so that some of the water content has a chance to soak into the wood. Only then should the acid be applied to the other half of the joint and the two brought together.

It is important that *sufficient* acid is applied. The only failure I ever had with this glue was the first time I used it. I did not allow for most of the hardener I applied soaking into the wood before I was able to bring the two pieces together. The 'acid' half of the joint must be shining and slick with moisture when brought into contact with the 'resin' half. Apply the acid liberally, therefore; you will certainly have some left in the bottle when all the tin of powder has been used.

After the resin is applied, the parts should be clamped in an immovable position within a maximum time of:
25 min. at a temperature of 15°C.
5 min. at a temperature of 30°C.
Clamps should be left on the joints for a minimum time of:
$3\frac{1}{2}$ hr. at a temperature of 15°C.
$1\frac{1}{4}$ hr. at a temperature of 30°C.

Clamping times should be doubled if the joints are likely to have to withstand strain as soon as they are removed. Full strength and water-resistance is not obtained until about 14 days after glueing.

It is worth noting that dry warm wood bonds better than cold damp wood, and it is as well to keep the parts in a warm dry atmosphere for some time before glueing.

Cascophen PC-1

Many boatbuilders use the resorcinol-phenol-formaldehyde and resorcinal-phenol type glues, either with or without heat, because of their rather better gap-filling qualities. Foreign matter such as china clay can be added to them to fill up the holes left by badly made joints. It is claimed that the adhesion is better if there is a gap to be filled, and this may well be so. To keep the waterproof qualities of the glue, however, mineral filler must not be used in a greater proportion than 40 parts to 100 parts of resin and 100 parts of hardener.

Both Aerodux 500 and Cascophen PC-1 resins, and their separate hardeners, are supplied in liquid form—the catalysts being alkaline rather than acidic. Resin and hardener are mixed together before application, and then applied to one or both surfaces, according to how good the joint is. On a badly fitting one, where surfaces do not touch everywhere, the glue is put on both.

Aerodux 500 has three grades of hardener—Fast, Medium and Slow. Extensive tables are available from the manufacturers for time factors over the three grades, but as a guide, the Medium grade hardener gives the mix a pot life of up to $5\frac{1}{2}$ hours at 15°C., and $1\frac{1}{2}$ hours at 30°C.

Using the Medium hardener, the parts must be assembled finally in
$2\frac{3}{4}$ hr. at a temperature of 15°C.
1 hr. at a temperature of 30°C.

Also with the Medium hardener cramps must remain on for a minimum time of
$8\frac{1}{2}$ hr. at a temperature of 15°C.
2 hr. at a temperature of 30°C.

The pot life of Cascophen after mixing with its hardener is 3 hours at 16°C. and $\frac{1}{2}$ hour at 32°C. Once it has been applied (to both surfaces) they must be assembled within about 10 minutes. Clamps must be left on for
5 hr. at a temperature of 16°C.
1 hr. at a temperature of 32°C.

Epoxide Resin Glues

Epoxy glues are sold in two parts, both very viscous substances. They are mixed together in equal parts. Most useful for our purpose is the Araldite handy pack, which is the AV 100 resin and the HV 100 hardener, in separate and different coloured tubes. For twenty or thirty pence, the pack goes a long way. Mixed at room temperatures, the usable life of small quantities of epoxy resin glue is about 4 hr. Curing time for Araldite is
24 hours at a temperature of 20°C.
3 hours at a temperature of 60°C.
20 minutes at a temperature of 100°C.

Clamping should only be light, in order not to starve the joint of glue.

Epoxide glues are particularly useful for bonding G.R.P. mouldings together and G.R.P. to wood, etc. They are more expensive for this type of application than is lamination by the use of glass and polyester resin, but there are circumstances where the latter method is not practical. Epoxide glues can be bought in large quantities direct from the factories, if required, but for our purposes the Handypack of Araldite is usually quite sufficient.

Deciding on the Glue

When deciding which glue to use, certain facts need to be taken into consideration. Urea formaldehyde glues are difficult to use with 'greasy' or resinous timbers such as teak, keruing and pitchpine. If thorough degreasing with Trichlorethylene is carried out, the faces of the joint roughened with coarse sand paper or, better, a hacksaw blade, and then degreased once more, these glues can be used. Higher pressures than normal should be used when clamping. It is better, however, to use resorcinol-formaldehyde glues with these and similar timbers.

Very dense woods, such as greenheart and lignum vitae cannot easily be glued with either the urea-formaldehyde or the resorcinol-phenol-formaldehyde types, the reason being that these dense timbers do not 'wet out', or soak away the moisture content of the resin. In these cases if glueing is necessary use an epoxide glue, but even so the surfaces must be roughened or scored thoroughly in order to provide a key.

Timbers slightly less dense, but still heavy—such as afrormosia, karri or oak, can be bonded with urea-formaldehyde or the resorcinol groups if both surfaces are well sanded and, after the resin is applied, some time allowed for evaporation before they are brought together. It is also helpful to use slightly higher pressures in cramping and, if possible, higher curing temperatures—up to about 60°C. Acid timbers, in particular, are more difficult to bond with the resorcinol glues because of the alkali nature of the glue. Urea-formaldehyde glues make it easier to bond such timbers, as the acid in them helps the catalyst process.

Staining

Acid in timber is the cause of staining, which can be a curse to the unwary. Oak, ash and some types of mahogany have high tannin content, and the acid in the urea-formaldehyde glues takes on an iron content if it comes into contact with ferrous metal. The iron in the glue then combines with the tannin in the wood to form an iron—tannin compound, which stains the wood. It is absolutely essential, then, to keep urea-formaldehyde glues away from iron or steel—no brush with metal parts should be used; there must be no iron nails or other fastenings in the wood; and neither resin nor hardener must be put in metal containers. Keep the glue well away from cramps and other tools, too.

If, in spite of all care, staining does occur, it can be removed with oxalic acid. But as this acid is not only highly corrosive but poisonous; and, moreover, may itself change the colour of some timbers, it is much better to leave it alone and make sure, instead, that no iron—tannin compounds form. If there are good reasons for using oxalic acid, it must be in a three per cent solution, applied with a pad; and an offcut of the stained wood should be tried out first. Also take great care to protect eyes, skin, clothes and food. Light-coloured and very porous materials are easily stained by the resorcinol glues, as they take up the alkali content, which is later leached out and shows up as dark patches. Try to avoid allowing this type of glue to 'run' unnecessarily over light-coloured, low density timbers such as agba.

Certain African hardwoods which are more readily obtainable these days than is teak, and somewhat cheaper, have interlocking grains. Afrormosia and iroko are examples, and these are often difficult to plane. Sometimes the grain tears up during planing, but more often it takes on a hard shine like case hardening, and must be well roughened before glueing in order to make a key. All shiny surfaces must be broken up, in fact, as must the surface of plywood where it is to be bonded. Plywood gets case hardened in the cutting and rolling machines, and then finally during heat setting.

Summing up on Glues

(a) Use epoxide glues—on our list Araldite or Epophen for bonding wood and other materials to G.R.P., unless laminating with tape and polyester resin. This depends largely on the area to be bonded, convenience, and expense.

(b) Do not use urea-formaldehyde glues—in our list Aerolite 306 with hardener—to bond greasy or resinous timbers. Use instead resorcinal or resorcinol-phenol-formaldehyde glues (Aerodux 500 or Cascophen). If only Aerolite is available, follow the degreasing instructions given earlier in this chapter.

(c) For very dense, heavy timbers bond with Araldite or Epophen.

(d) Acid woods such as oak should be bonded with acid resin glues—the urea formaldehyde types, Aerolite 306 in our list.

(e) Prevent staining of woods containing tannin by preventing the glue coming into contact with ferrous metal. Keep the resorcinols from unnecessary contact with light-coloured, porous woods.

(f) It is best to be on the safe side and keep all resin glues from contact with metals—brushes, containers, fittings, etc.

Skin Protection

When using resins, it is easy to get dermatitis; once it dries on the hands, it is extremely difficult to remove. Keep a wet swab handy when glueing, and wipe the fingers continually. Also use a barrier cream.

Other Glues

The only other types of glue we shall have much to do with are those based on rubber—the contact and pressure-sensitive glues. Evostik, Bostik and Dunlop are all good glues, and it is only a matter of passing interest, I suppose, that a rubber plantation would disown them on sight. They are basically mixtures of natural and synthetic rubbers, both altered out of all molecular recognition in the laboratory. They were discovered when chemists experimented with breaking down old rubber, such as worn-out tyres, for re-use. We can use them for bonding melamine sheets to wood, soft plastics to G.R.P., etc. They are only really effective, in my experience, where large flat areas have to be stuck together.

Carpentry Tools

Glues are important tools, but in order to make the furniture and fittings which will improve the G.R.P. yacht, we also need wood-cutting and wood-shaping tools. The improvements described in the following chapters would be possible—just—with nothing more than a good saw, a couple of chisels, a carpenter's brace, one or two twist drills, and reams of sandpaper. But to make life easy, a rather larger kit is advisable : just how large depends very much on where the work will be carried out. Major alterations to my own glass fibre sloop have been made during the winter, when the yacht is standing in a field about thirty miles from home. No power is available, and working conditions are primitive. A pile of old railway sleepers as an outdoor bench, and a short plank between the bunks as a sawhorse in the cabin. It is essential, of course, that most of the work is done where the boat is, as it needs to be offered up continually to make sure that edges fit neatly into all the compound curves of the hull.

Sometimes, however, when timber needs reducing considerably, or there are dozens of holes to drill, or a big sanding job, I take the work home and use power tools.

A Reasonable Kit

The kit I carry down to the boat each week is a minimum one. I have a list pinned up in the shed at home to make sure that everything needed goes into the bag on a Saturday morning. I learned to take that much trouble the hard way—getting all the way down to the boat only to find that I had forgotten the most important tool needed that day.

The kit consists of handsaw, tenon saw, keyhole saw. Metal square and several pencils. Six wood chisels from $\frac{1}{4}$ in. to $1\frac{1}{2}$ in. in quarter inch steps. Mallet, claw hammer. Assorted screwdrivers, including a small electrician's, a heavy long-shafted one and, most important, two short dumpy ones. These are only about $2\frac{1}{2}$ in. long and can be got into all sorts of awkward places where longer shafts would not go. One has a chisel blade, the other fits Phillips screws, and both have thick, easy to grip handles.

Then there is a twist drill with $\frac{1}{2}$ in. chuck and a complete range of twist bits. A metal rebate plane with an inch wide blade and a removable fence, so that it doubles as a smoothing plane. A long Surform. Tinsnips, pliers, pincers, sanding block and range of papers from fine to coarse. Very important too is a marking gauge and a sharp knife. (The knife I use fits the same handle as the keyhole saw, and is housed inside the handle when the saw is in use.) A flexible rule is, of course, an absolute necessity.

At home I keep an electric drill with a portable circular saw device, sanding discs and a carbide tungsten cutting disc, all backed by a rubber arbor. I also have a number of other unlikely tools, bought on the spur of the moment or given as birthday presents. There is a set of hole-cutting saws, for example. They have been in the shed for years, and I have used the largest only, and only once—when making a cup rack for the boat. I could have used the keyhole saw instead ; the hole saw was quicker and neater, but I cannot claim that it has paid for itself.

One tool not mentioned above because it comes in a slightly different category, but absolutely essential just the same, is a work-holding vice. The one I use is kept on board permanently; being made of light alloy, it is rustproof. The jaws are adjustable and designed to hold any shape of work, are provided with slip-on plastic sheaths for wood, and the instrument will fasten to either vertical or horizontal ledges, besides having a suction pad which, the manufacturer claimed, enable it to be attached to any smooth surface.

This is a good idea, as there are lots of smooth surfaces on a boat. The trouble is that when working with any length of wood over a foot long, too much leverage is applied for the suction pad to cope with.

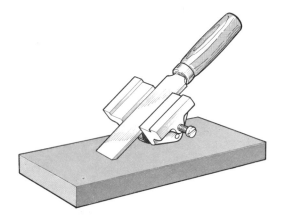

Fig. 1

Expert Sharpening

A more annoying fault is that, although the vice is made of corrosion proof alloy, the bolts with which the various pieces are held together are mild steel. I found this out when they had rusted solid; they were eventually freed and replaced with stainless steel—but this is an example of carelessness on the part of many manufacturers. I should emphasize that this vice is sold as being of particular use to boat owners—and so it is, now that I have discarded the suction pad and use the screw-up clamp provided.

Another item which should be included by all except the man with a natural flair, is a honing guide. The less expert one is with edged tools, the more they will need to be sharpened—and paradoxically enough, the less sharpening they will get. Watch the expert. He sharpens chisels and plane irons often, but the amateur plods along with blunt tools, making hard work of everything he does. The amateur's trouble is that, when sharpening, he cannot judge the correct angle of the blade to the stone, and cannot hold it there even if he gets it. The result being that he often finishes with a worse edge than when he started.

In the first place, unless the tools are new and unused, they should be professionally ground. Chisels and plane irons usually have two bevels, the long one being ground on a sandstone. Having got this, it is a simple matter to keep the second bevel, the short one, keen with a honing guide. This is a gadget which grips the blade of plane or chisel in such a way that it is held against the oilstone at the correct angle. All the operator has to do is apply some pressure and push the tool back and forth (Fig. 1).

To go with this, of course, an oilstone is needed—a good one. Cheap stones soon wear into grooves. A double-sided one is useful, with coarse and fine surfaces, both of which must be used with a fine lubricating oil. Under no circumstances use engine or other thick oil. To use the honing guide effectively, keep the fingers of one hand low down on the blade, holding it firmly but not with too much pressure, against the surface of the oilstone. Move the guide, on its roller, back and forth with the other hand. Rub until a thin, turned-back edge can be felt on the reverse side of the blade; this is known as a 'wire edge', and is removed by rubbing the back of the tool flat across the stone, then slicing the edge across a piece of waste wood.

Chisels and plane irons are usually honed at an angle of either 25 or 30 degrees. It is important to hone at the same angle as that already on the iron.

Home Made Cramps

Sharp or blunt, tools are used to make or alter things; and somewhere along the line glue will be used, as we have already seen. Which means that cramps will be needed to hold the pieces tight together until the glue has set. Some jobs seem to need a great many cramps, particularly if curved surfaces are to be held together, and they would be an expensive item were it not possible to make some very effective G-cramps from what is virtually scrap wood. Any number can be made, and used in conjunction with not more than two pairs of bought cramps.

Fig. 2 shows how they are made. They can be of varying jaw widths and depths, as required, and made of plywood for strength. The cramps should be about half an inch thick, so several thicknesses of thinner ply can be glued together for each one. As long as the faces of the jaws are parallel, the actual outline of the cramp is immaterial, as to shape and finish.

Long wedges are used to tighten the work in them, and wide packing pieces used between jaw and work surface to prevent the latter being marked. Bought G-cramps are used to cramp down the glued pieces, the home-made cramp wedged into place alongside, then the bought one taken off and used elsewhere.

Another and very simple type of cramp, useful for holding glued blocks in place, etc., is made from two pieces of hardwood with a bolt through their centres. They can be of any length and thickness; the longer the thicker; but pieces about a foot long should have a section of roughly an inch square.

The bolt is unscrewed until the distance between the two parallel lengths is the same as the thickness of the work to be held. This is placed between the jaws at one end, and packing pieces and wedges driven in at the other end provide, through leverage about the bolt as a pivot, the necessary pressure on the work (Fig. 3.)

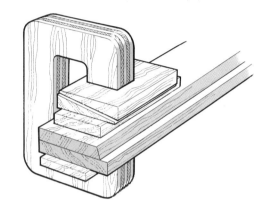

Fig. 2

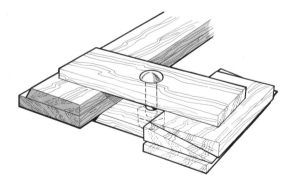

Fig. 3

Screwdrivers   I have already mentioned the importance I place upon screwdrivers. There is nothing uglier, nor more troublesome, than the torn head of a wood screw. Moreover, the man who finds difficulty in driving screws soon becomes tired of the chore, and is likely to tell himself that the job does not really call for so many as he thought it did. Often with unfortunate results.

The use of the correct and properly sharpened tool is a revelation. One screwdriver will *not* do for almost every size of screw, to start with. The width of the blade must not be greater than the diameter of the head of the screw; and it should be a fraction thinner than the width of the slot. (If it is thicker, it will not enter properly, and ruin the head.)

It is a good idea to have at least three different types of handle, each with its own set of interchangeable blades. But do not buy cheap screwdrivers, the blades of which become blunted and twisted after one use. For the blades must be kept as sharp and trim as chisel blades. Sharpening is best done on a hand-turned, slow-speed grindstone; the edge of the blade must be absolutely straight, not curved away at the corners. And the sides of the blade should be hollow ground—nearly everyone allows them to become convex, which is entirely wrong, as the bulge encourages the blade to slip out of the slot.

Among a screwdriver kit it is a good idea to have a powerful yankee, or pump screwdriver; this can take a lot of the hard work out of driving a number of small to medium length screws. But where quantities of longish screws have to be driven home, such as when building a wooden dinghy, buy a set of blades to fit an ordinary carpenter's brace. This allows a good steady force to be applied to the head of the screw, at a controlled pace.

4 Using wood to improve G.R.P. Simple mistakes. Simple joints. The art of drilling and screwing and using stops. Disguising the screw heads and filling up holes. The correct way to cut Formica and similar decorative plastics—and the secret of sticking them down with contact glues.

Because improving a G.R.P. yacht necessitates making things to fit it, I want to explain a few more ideas which I consider basic. It may seem that although I purport to be writing about glass fibre, most of what I have said so far, and am still saying, is to do with wood. This, I am afraid, is unavoidable. For 75 per cent of the ways of embellishing a G.R.P. boat consist of adding to its bareness the beauty of fine wood.

Although we may be rank amateurs, it is difficult not to shudder when we see the mess which another amateur has made of his yacht on an adjacent mooring. And it is true that people do make a pig's breakfast of work, when:

(a) they are unaware of the short cuts possible with modern materials;

(b) they have not tried at all for line or shape, but only for utility; and

(c) not nearly enough pure thought has been put into the job.

I shall reiterate the necessity for thought at frequent intervals. It is the ability to think which puts the yacht owner on a plane above that occupied by the slasher of railway carriage seats, for example.

When a decision has been taken to make something, sit down and think about it before taking up a single tool. About how this 'thing' should look when it is finished. About the process of making it. Then try to project what it will actually look like when it is made according to the ideas which thought has constructed up to this point. Be honest, and admit that it will probably appear nothing like the original concept.

So do we compromise, or try to do better? Think about ways in which something nearer the original ideal could be attained—a different type of fastening, a different bonding method. They may appear beyond present skills—but if further thought is given to the project, stage by stage, it is almost certain that a way will be found.

I discovered early on in my own saga of improvements another important reason for thought—that without it I could make a stupid mistake in measurement, or a saw cut on the wrong face of the work piece, or drill holes too deep. So I gradually got into the habit of marking the wood and then, before picking up saw or chisel, stopping to think about what I intended to do. Holding the wood up, mentally, in the position for which it was designed, and making a mental joint. And then making the measurements all over again. Even so, I still made mistakes fairly often. But over all, I must have saved quite a considerable sum on wood not ruined, and even more wear on my temper. An example of the very real benefit of giving plenty of time to thought occurred when I was making a sliding hatch for the coachroof. Two side strips met on a corner at a compound angle; the angle was less than 90 degrees, and while one side was vertical, the other was a few degrees off vertical.

It seemed to me that this joint needed a dovetail, both for the sake of appearance and strength—one edge had to be pulled to close the hatch, and I had not so much faith in resin glues then, as I have since gained. But I could not help feeling that a hidden dovetail in a comparatively small space and at such angles was beyond my capabilities. The friend with whom I was working thought so too— just glue it and screw it was his recommendation.

But when he had gone home that evening, I sat in the cabin and thought about the joint and the angles. I got a scrap of paper and a pencil and scribbled. It took me an hour to be sure—but then I picked up the saw and chisel and made the joint. I won't claim it was perfect. But the angles were right, all of them. And the joint, filled a little with glue and sawdust, looked fine. It still does.

In most of the carpentry jobs we do on the yacht joints, as I said before, are not absolutely essential. To be able to make simple joints, however, not only improves workmanship, it adds inherent strength and sometimes enables a much neater and more compact job to be made. It is a good idea to know how to make at least two joints.

Mortise and Tenon

Used mostly when making frames—for doors, for the sides of lockers, etc. There are two side pieces, called stiles, in which are made the mortises, or holes, and a top and bottom rail, on which are cut the tenons, or tongues (Fig. 4). The width of the wood is marked off from each end of the rails and the thickness of the tongue (which should be gauged to the width of a suitable available chisel) marked out.

Cut carefully with a tenon saw down each side of the tenon and across the shoulders, keeping outside the marks. Then, using a drill slightly smaller than the chisel, drill right through the stile, clearing out afterwards with the chisel, and keeping always just inside the marks. The shaded areas in the drawing show the waste material.

An aid to making this type of joint is a mortise marking gauge, which has two adjustable scribing points, instead of the usual one. Use of this means that all the limit lines for the joints will always be in the same place. But in fact, even if you have never made a mortise and tenon joint before, two or three practice attempts on scrap wood will find the veriest amateur as proficient as need be. Remembering that even the experts use wedges for tightening loose joints, and that resin glues will take up any remaining slack.

**Dovetail
Joints**

There are various types of dovetail joint, but all are merely variations
on the simple through dovetail. Make sure that the ends to be jointed
are planed square, then mark a line from the end of each the same
distance as the thickness of the wood (Fig. 5). Mark in the position
of the dovetails on Part A; the only criterion for these is that they are
best if they are evenly spaced, and the neck of each tail should be
wide enough so that it will not easily break off when being worked.
This is according to the strength of the wood, and one's own
judgment. The ideal slope is to the ratio of $\frac{5}{8}$ in. to 3 in.

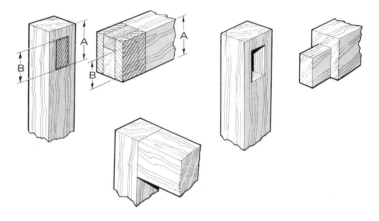

Fig. 4   Mortise and tenon joint

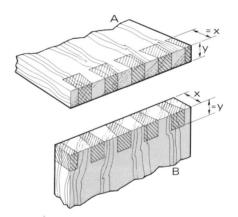

Fig. 5   Simple through dovetail

Sawcuts are made from the ends of the wood and along the shoulders, sawing outside the lines, and the intermediate waste is chiselled out. Chisel half way through from one side, then turn the wood over and work from the other side.

When the waste from A has been removed, put B in the vice, lay A on top of it, and mark around the wedges with a sharp pencil. In this way, if the tails have not been made perfectly regular, the irregularity is transferred to B and a better fit obtained than if both pieces were marked at the same time and then cut without reference to each other. Saw down from the end and chisel out the waste.

Good dovetails are not quite so simple to make as mortise and tenon joints, but practice makes perfect, and there is great satisfaction in getting them right. If more information is needed than that given here—this is not intended to be a treatise on carpentry, but only to whet the appetite—buy 'Teach Yourself Carpentry' by Charles Hayward.

Inserting Screws

One of the boatbuilder's favourite types of fastening is the barbed nail, a very secure device but one which, from the amateur's point of view, has one drawback. If put in the wrong place, withdrawal is difficult and results in some damage to the surrounding wood.

Glue and screw is undoubtedly the type of fastening we shall use most often in improving the glass fibre yacht; but unfortunately the art of driving in screws is often approached in far too light-hearted a manner. It seems too simple. Anyone can put in a screw. But can they?

In the first place, it is necessary to examine the work. When fastening any two pieces of wood together on a boat, the chances of both having parallel sides are quite remote. One will usually be wedge—or some other shape. Before going ahead like a bull at a gate, it is necessary to decide at which angle to insert the screw— and the answer in every case is that the surface of the screw head must be parallel and on the same plane with the surface of the top layer of wood—that into which it will be countersunk.

Drilling

No screw should ever be driven into wood before holes have first been drilled to take it. 'Holes' in the plural, because three are needed for each screw; one of the necessary depth and diameter to take the thread; one of the correct depth and diameter to take the shank—the upper, smooth shaft of the screw; and a third to take the head of the screw.

When driving large numbers of screws of the same size, it is a good idea to have at least two, and if possible three, hand drills on the go. For this sort of job I usually have an ordinary wheel-type hand drill for the smallest size bit, to take the thread; a mains electric drill if I am at home, or one operated from a 12-volt battery if I am on the boat, to drill the shank hole. And an ordinary carpenter's brace for the countersink bit. This arrangement saves a lot of time in changing over different bits into the same drill, as it is often not possible to drill all of one size hole at once.

Mild steel screws should never be used in marine work, of course.

Nor should brass: corrosion causes the zinc to leach out of brass very quickly, the resultant fastening being something of the consistency of gruyere cheese, with about as much strength. Use gunmetal or monel metal.

When putting screws into hardwoods, such as mahogany and teak, there is always the danger of splitting it, so the drilled holes should be only slightly smaller than the screws they are to take. In soft wood, the holes can be proportionately smaller. Using, say, a 6 gauge screw, I would use a $\frac{3}{32}$ in. bit in mahogany, and a $\frac{1}{16}$ in. bit in soft wood, for the thread. In both cases the second hole, for the shank, needs to be $\frac{5}{32}$ in. The countersink must make a shallow indent, only a fraction larger than the screw head, and it must be dropped deep enough to take stopping.

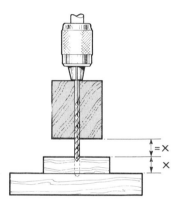

Fig. 6   Control of length of a drilled hole: shaded block stops drill at desired point

Before drilling for screws it is more than worthwhile to make stops to prevent drilling too deep. If the thread hole is to be, say, 1 in. deep, cut a block of wood about 2 in. square and drill a hole through its centre with the bit to be used. The block should be of such a thickness that, when it is right up to the chuck, exactly 1 in. of twist drill protrudes on the other side. The bit itself can be adjusted in the chuck to get this measurement correct.

A punch mark should always be made in the work; locate the punch mark with the tip of the bit, then drill until the stop comes down to meet the work. Use of such a stop has the added advantage that its flat underside comes against the surface being drilled, and helps to ensure that the hole is drilled at right-angles to it.

An alternative stop can be made by two flat pieces of wood,

about $1\frac{1}{2}$ in. long and $\frac{1}{2}$ in. wide, bolted together around the twist bit, positioned the correct distance from the tip of the drill to ensure the depth of hole required. The only advantage of this type of stop is that it can be adjusted for different hole depths. The disadvantage is that, however much care is used, when the stop meets the work there will be a fraction of a second when the drill is penetrating the stop. So that constant checking of distance is necessary.

Covering the Heads

The screws having been inserted correctly, and correctly counter-sunk, their heads have to be covered. It is a great mistake to make a poor job of it, for this is where even the amateur carpenter can give his work a professional look.

In the first place, it is, of course, a mistake to use anything other than the best woods obtainable; mahogany, teak, or at the very least, afrormosia. Pine and deal are cheaper; but for the sake of even a few pounds, it is not worth trying to be economic in this direction. The beautiful grain of mahogany, the ship like appearance of teak, cannot be duplicated, and it is as well to ignore advertisements which try to persuade the gullible that this or that preparation offers a glorious finish to softwood making it indistinguishable from the real thing. Cheap wood stained looks like cheap wood stained, no matter how it may be dressed up.

Using expensive wood, then, it is equally a mistake to spoil it by using synthetic filler to cover screw heads. Cover them with the same wood as that from which the item is made.

First obtain some scrap pieces of metal pipe, an inch or two long each, of inside diameters about the same as the diameters of the heads of the screws in use. Steel pipe is best, but in these small sizes it will probably be necessary to use copper heating pipe. The next item is a countersink bit of the same diameter as the inside diameter of the pipe. Sharpen the rim of one end of the pipe with files—a thin rat tail for the inside, and a fine half round to take the burr off the outside of the circumference. Then using scrap pieces of the wood being worked, punch out some discs. Put the sharpened end of the pipe on the surface of the wood, and give the other end a sharp blow with a hammer.

The discs need be no thicker than $\frac{1}{16}$ in., and faced marine plywood is probably the best material from which to cut them, splitting away a couple of the veneers with a sharp chisel. The discs will jam inside the pipe, and will have to be pushed out carefully with a ram. Quite a few will break, but as the wood being used is only scrap, this does not really matter.

Having obtained a sufficient supply of discs, fill the hole above the screw head with glue, press the disc down on to it, and wipe away the surplus. If using a two-part glue, I stand the discs in a saucer in which there is a thin film of acid, and put the paste on to the screws. Line the grain of the discs up with the grain of the wood in which they are set. Rub down with fine sandpaper just before the glue finally sets. The dust will combine with the glue and fill any slight irregularities around the rim of the disc.

Stoppers

For stopping gaps in badly made joints which will not be visible, but where ones conscience would worry if something were not done about them, there are several very good plastic putties on the market—materials which not only make good the faults, but impart strength, too. There is one, for example, called Plastic Padding ; and there are plenty of other resin putties.

For covering screw heads where they don't show, and so where there is little point in using discs, plastic wood filler, Brummer stopping, or one of the many similar preparations, are quite adequate.

A great deal of marine plywood is used in and on boats, and in my opinion marine grade ply should always be used even in interior joinery work. Damp lies everywhere in a boat. Marine grade plywood is bonded with waterproof and boil proof resins, and should never delaminate even if the boat sinks ; whereas cheaper interior grades are very likely to split into their component veneers when the damp air gets at them.

However, if well protected with varnish or paint, some people see no harm in using interior grades for certain purposes—such as backing lockers. Whatever sort of plywood is used, it is absolutely essential that its edges are properly stopped. Most damage is done to plywood by moisture soaking into the wood between the glue layers, entering through soft grain ends. It is little use having glues with giant strength if the wood they are holding disintegrates.

Always, therefore, fill the edge of plywood panels before the final sanding is done. Polyester resin, some preparation such as Ronseal, or even varnish, will do. Let this soak well into the rough ends, and harden off. Then sandpaper smooth, and apply more filler or sealant, finally varnishing or painting.

Melamine Plastics

A number of jobs being done in the interior will be improved with the use of melamine laminates—Formica and the like. But they are not quite as proof against burns, cuts and stains as was claimed for them when they first came on the market. But they do have these resistant properties to a higher degree than most materials—and generally speaking, the better known (and more expensive) makes of melamine sheets have these attributes to a better degree than the cheaper sorts.

Melamine sheets are brittle—and although they can be cut with a fine-toothed saw by the expert, the amateur nearly always manages to chip the edge of the top, most important surface. The tool I use is the Stanley Formica blade, which fits into that firm's padsaw handle. It is a double-edged blade, with a hook, and it cuts in the same way that a glass cutter cuts glass. Curves and compound curves can be cut, simply by tracing over the outline with the point of the blade.

Because melamine is such a smooth substance, the knife will very easily wander from the outline, so several passes are best ; the first done very lightly and carefully, just scratching the surface. The second pass can have more pressure behind it, because the point now has a groove to follow. Straight lines, of course, should be followed with a straight-edge, but care still has to be taken that the point does not wander.

When the outline has been evenly scored, hold the material each side of and close to the line, with the first finger and thumb of each hand, and break upwards, folding the hard surface of the material on to itself. Follow carefully along the curves, breaking a few inches at a time.

For sticking the plastic to the wooden surface, many people recommend a urea glue, which has the advantage that the melamine sheet can be moved about until properly aligned. It then has to be clamped down, with even pressure all over the surface, until the glue sets. This is not always easy to achieve. Personally, I always use impact glue, so that complete adhesion is obtained as soon as the surfaces touch.

Both surfaces must be clean and dry, and the glue applied evenly to both of them, all over. They must then be left to dry. Where failure with contact glues occurs, it is usually because (a) the surfaces were greasy or (b) the impatient user does not allow both surfaces to dry to the point where there is no tackiness at all left to the touch. Avoid getting them greasy when testing with the fingers.

Contact glues can be infuriating in the difficulty of getting the melamine aligned properly with the wood as they come together. Once they touch, there is no separating them again; but a fraction of an inch out, unnoticed at the starting end, can result in a huge discrepancy when smoothing hands reach the other end of the sheet.

The secret of avoiding this is very simple, and is possible because both surfaces, being completely dry, will stick to nothing but each other.

Completely cover the lower, or fixed surface, with sheets of newspaper. If it is a vertical surface, such as a bulkhead, tack the paper at the top with small pieces of Scotch tape. Now put the melamine surface on to, or against, the fixed surface—the paper will stick to neither. Align the plastic sheet with the wood by feel through the paper; press firmly in the middle of the sheet to hold it in position, then draw out one sheet of newspaper. Press the melamine down, smoothing out towards the edges to expel pockets of air, and it is now held securely and in the correct alignment. Withdraw the remainder of the paper, sheet by sheet, smoothing out the air as you go.

5 More details of fastenings and their use. Sealing raw edges. Making use of more than one method of fastening for the same job. Temporary supports.

We now have the necessary tools, and some knowledge of how to use them in order to make improvements to a small G.R.P. yacht. Whatever we do or make will mean bonding or fastening in some way to the hull; it has already been shown that there are, contrary to popular opinion, several ways of accomplishing this, and the present short chapter will explain more fully these methods, which can be used separately or in conjunction.

Through-bolting
The first and most simple method is direct through bolting. This can be used wherever both sides of the work are accessible; it cannot be used through a moulded-in deckhead lining, for example, as it is not possible to get into the space between deckhead and lining. But it can be used through the deck for fastening on deck equipment above—cleats and winches, and anything which must be securely fastened down. A handrail in the cabin, fastened to an unlined deckhead, should be bolted through. Generally speaking, however, no-one wants to spoil the fair lines of hull, or clutter deck or coach-roof, with protruding boltheads. So that where equipment is to be fixed to the inside of the hull, methods other than bolts are generally used.

On the occasions when bolts are inserted through hull or deck, a layer of waterproof material must be interposed between the fitting and the hull. This can be one of the mastic compounds—very sticky, doughy materials which harden on the surface, when exposed to the air, but retain some inner resilience for a long time. Or it can be one of the new sealants obtainable in sheet form, less messy to use, but effective none the less. The sheet is cut to the exact shape of the fitting, and holes cut in it to take the bolts. It is a good idea to use it inside, too, between the hull and the bearing pad. For our purpose bolts will nearly always be used through internal bulkheads or through G.R.P. joining lips, such as that formed where the coachroof is bonded to the deck.

The important thing to remember when using bolts is that it is absolutely essential to use as large a bearing plate as possible behind the fibre glass. This is necessary to spread the load, for even if there does not appear to be much of a strain on the shelf or whatever is to be attached to the G.R.P. bulkhead, allowances must always be made for the unexpected. The man who loses his balance when the deck heels, invariably grabs for the first hand hold. Your shelf, secured only by a nut, will pull right out as soon as this happens, and cause considerable damage to the bulkhead at the same time.

The pad behind the G.R.P. need not be heavy, but its area should be as large as possible up to the size of the fitting it is supporting. It may be of plywood, or of light metal such as aluminium; but in the latter case the pad should be bonded on to the panel, completely encased in resin and glass, in order to insulate it from the harder metal of the holding bolts. This is done in order to prevent electrolysis between the dissimilar metals. The bolts should be of non-corrosive metal, such as gunmetal.

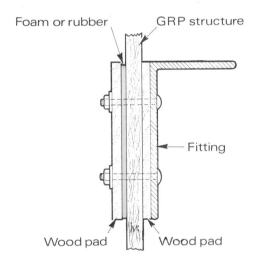

Fig. 7   Securing a fitting to G.R.P.

A pressure pad should also be used immediately under the fitting, if this does not provide its own large area in contact with the bulkhead. The G.R.P. is thus sandwiched between two pads, and its holding strength is thereby much increased. If curvature of the hull makes overall pressure pads impossible, then strips, or individual pads for each bolt, must be used, these being as large as practical.

It is also a good idea to insert a layer of resilient material between the bearing pad and the bulkhead; plastic foam, sheet rubber, or even mastic compound will do. This helps to prevent too great pressure being put on the bolts, which can damage the G.R.P. by crushing. (Fig. 7)

Raw Edges

It has already been explained exactly how G.R.P. is moulded, and that it consists of resin and thousands of fine glass fibres mixed up together. It will be appreciated, then, that when a hole is drilled through a G.R.P. panel, the raw ends, of glass fibres will be exposed. These can draw in moisture by capilliary action—moisture from the atmosphere, which is often saturated in the cabin of a boat. Whenever a hole is drilled, therefore, these raw edges should be sealed— ideally with resin, but in the case of small bolt or screw holes, they can be sealed with mastic, or even rubber-based glue.

Wood Screws

It is sometimes quite permissible, when little weight is involved, to use ordinary wood screws, driven through into wooden pads. At one time I put up a row of hooks on a bulkhead in this way—drilling holes slightly larger than the screw threads through a strip of $\frac{1}{4}$ in. plywood 18 in. long and 3 in. wide. This was held in its proposed position against the bulkhead, and the holes continued through the G.R.P. panel.

Someone was then deputized to stand on the other side of the bulkhead, holding a $\frac{1}{2}$ in. strip of hardwood behind it, and the hooks were screwed home into that. The hooks held nothing heavy and remained secure as long as I needed them there. Hooks with collars at the throat were used, by the way, in order to keep the outside plywood strip firmly in position against the panel. This saved having to glue it.

Rawlnuts

Many small G.R.P. yachts are made with a separately moulded G.R.P. headliner. This is designed to cut down condensation, which is as much of a problem in fibreglass as it is in steel hulls. The headliner is usually bonded into position inside the coachroof before the latter goes on; naturally, the space between liner and coachroof is minute, usually no more than $\frac{1}{4}$ in. at the outside, and of course it is quite inaccessible once the boat is built.

The headliner is normally a very thin moulding, and it would be dangerous to put excessive weight on it. But it is quite strong enough to support, say, a net into which to stow the ensign, or the skipper's woollen hat—if there were any way of rigging a net to it.

There are, in fact, at least two possible ways of doing just that. One is by the use of Rawlnuts, which are bolts carrying their own pressure pads. Rawlnuts, made in various sizes and lengths and available in every ironmongery, are by the Rawlplug people; dome-headed bolts of non-corrosive metal, carrying a washer just under the head and a nut at the far end. Nut and washer are joined by a slim rubber sleeve.

A hole of just sufficient diameter to take the sleeve is drilled through the object to be fastened and the deckhead, panel or bulkhead to which it will be fixed. The Rawlnut is pushed through. When the head is turned with a screwdriver, the sleeve cannot turn because of friction with the side of the hole; and the nut at the end cannot turn because it is fixed to the sleeve. The nut therefore makes its way up the shaft of the threaded bolt. In doing so, it compresses the rubber sleeve from end to end; and being rubber, the sleeve takes the path of least resistance and swells outwards—behind the panel, thus forming a small but resilient and strong bearing surface behind the G.R.P. The Rawlnut is mainly useful for holding small and lightweight fittings; but it can also be used in conjunction with other methods of fastening, as will be seen presently.

Glue

The second method of fastening to thin panels such as deckheads, to which there is no access from the rear, is by means of adhesive. The correct adhesive to use for this is an epoxy resin, two-part product such as Araldite.

There are several points to note when using this type of glue to bond to G.R.P., and although these have been mentioned in a previous chapter, they cannot be stressed too much. One is that both surfaces to be joined must be clean and free from grease (but this applies to all glues). A thin layer of grease from the release agent used when the hull was moulded can remain for years, and this must be thoroughly cleaned off. The surface of the G.R.P. must also be roughened with an instrument such as the tang of a file or the corner of a chisel. The smaller the bearing surface, the more important is this roughening process. The treatment of the wood surface to be attached to the G.R.P. has already been dealt with.

The epoxy glue is mixed carefully in the proportions as instructed, applied, and then held under slight pressure in position for a period of time which varies according to ambient temperature, as we have already seen. This is where the aid of a Rawlnut may well come in, as it can be used to hold a fitting in place while the glue sets. It may subsequently be removed, or left where it is as an added safeguard.

Resin and Tape

The classical method of joining things to a G.R.P. hull must, of course, be the use of G.R.P. itself—resin and glass. It is worth repeating here that the equipment needed is resin—probably bought in pint cans—the correct hardener or catalyst—and woven glass tape at least 2 in. wide. Other equipment needed is a jar or plastic cup for mixing resin and catalyst; a measuring jar calibrated in some way to make it easy to draw off correct quantities; and either a syringe or eye dropper; a mixing spatula; sharp scissors for cutting the tape; a brush with which to apply the resin; a narrow wooden roller of the type which decorators use to tamp down the edges of wall-paper; and a tin containing solvent for cleaning the brush and roller after use.

A Small Locker

Do not mix resin and hardener until all other preparations are complete. We will suppose that a small locker is being fitted against the side of the hull. The hull cannot be drilled through, so neither bearing pads nor Rawlnuts can be used through that. The top of the locker comes up against the deck head liner, however, so we can give some support by fastening upwards with small Rawlnuts, at the same time shoring from below with timber. The sides of the locker have had their rear edges shaped to follow the curvature of the side of the hull, so there can be no back to it. Hold the locker in the position to which it is to be fixed and run a pencil around the rear edge, all round, marking its outline on the hull. Now drill holes for the Rawlnuts through the top of the locker and through the deckhead lining; screw home the Rawlnuts to make sure they fit, and will tighten, then remove them again.

Put the locker to one side, and prepare to tackle the most difficult but most important part of this method of fastening. Difficult in the sense of tedious and long, and therefore only too easy to skimp.

A band an inch wide around the inside of the pencil mark on the hull must be thoroughly cleaned and roughened. First, scrape off all paint—the inside of G.R.P. hulls is often coated with emulsion paint— then clean with turpentine or white spirit. Tetrachloride is better, but not safe to use in confined spaces. Next, roughen the area with some suitable tool. I have never come across anything which will do the job easily; I usually get by with a rasp, the corner of a broken hacksaw blade, the corner of an old chisel, or something similar.

Whatever is used, the job is not simple, because properly cured polyester resin is rock hard and as smooth as glass. It must be done, however. Get through the surface of the resin until the tool starts to catch and bring up short fibres from the glass mat lay up. Not just in one place, but all over the inch-wide band. This makes certain of a good key to which the new resin will bond. An inch-wide band around the inside of the back of the locker must also be roughened up. Although wood is porous, the grain may be filled with grease from handling or, if it is plywood, have been case-hardened during the manufacturing process.

The next step is to cut eight lengths of the glass tape, so that we can bond on two layers all round. Now the locker is offered up again, shored up from below, and the Rawlnuts screwed home. Rawlnuts into the deckhead lining are an aid to security, but not sufficient on their own unless the locker is very light weight indeed. Shoring from below must be properly done, for if it should come away before the resin is set, and the locker shifts, the whole process will have to be started all over again.

Mix the resin to the exact proportions instructed by the manu-facturers or suppliers (first protecting the hands with a good barrier cream) then take a cheap but clean 1-in. paint brush and apply the resin liberally to the combined 2-in. band on hull and locker. Put the tape, length by length, in position along the seam, holding one end of each length steady and stroking it down with the brush, using gentle motions away from the anchored end. Then pass the brush over the tape again, this time using a short jabbing or stippling motion to drive out any air pockets.

When the tape is neatly in position all round, apply more resin and the second layer of tape. It is important, however many layers are used, always to put the resin on first, then brush the tape down on to it. In this case, two layers should be sufficient, but if no secondary support, such as Rawlnuts, is used, then one can be on the safe side and use three. Put each succeeding layer of tape on while the resin from the previous one is still tacky.

Leave any temporary support in place as long as possible—at least 48 hours—so that the resin has time to cure. Curing time depends largely on factors outside our control—temperature, humidity, and so on. If the roughening was done thoroughly and the resin and catalyst proportions mixed correctly, the locker will become as much part of the hull as though it were moulded in in the first place.

When the resin is properly cured, sandpaper over it to remove stray strands of glass, inadvertent creases, and so on. The inside of the locker may then be painted or varnished. I once used polyurethane varnish over tape which had cured for a week and was bone hard— and the resin softened up again and the whole thing had to be stripped off. The manufacturers told me that there was no reason for this, but it happened. So I advise no polyurethane varnish on top of recent resin, anyway.

A locker has been used as an example of a method of bonding, but this can be used for almost any type of addition in a G.R.P. yacht.

6 Repairs to the hull, professional *v.* handyman. Scratches, impact damage. Cutting away the fractured material and replacing with a fair repair. Finishing off.

One of the sales points used by the builders of glass fibre hulls is that they are much more simple to repair than are wooden yachts. Much prejudice remains, for has not everyone hammered a nail into a piece of wood? Even the man with no skill as a shipwright can see what is involved in taking out a plank, replacing a cracked frame. But glass and resin. . . . This material would seem to need a scientist.

Some repair yards also take this attitude, judging by the charges they make for this type of work. But basically, the salesmen are right; it *is* easy for the owner to make his own repairs—usually much easier than with a wooden hull. Success depends on doing the job correctly; and although the tyro may not get a perfect flow of line as the professional does, it will really depend on just how much effort he is prepared to put in. As with everything else, practice makes perfect. Unless he is a very careless or unfortunate boat owner he is not, however, likely to get much chance to practice on his own craft. So he must do the best he can.

Yachts in Hazard
Nevertheless, the only yachts which never sustain any damage are those kept in the back garden on a trailer for twelve months of the year, and never under any circumstances taken near the water. Even then tiles, chimneys and trees may possibly fall on them! Not every yacht will need a major repair though there will always be cases of ugly looking holes in topsides caused by collision in congested waters or even by one mishandled yacht to another lying on her mooring, more often there will be scrapes which expose the hull under the gel coat, or fittings torn off which in turn will damage the G.R.P. lay up or structure. With a conventional wooden hull, each member involved in the damage, some of them extending into other parts of the hull, has to be tediously removed. With G.R.P. we are only concerned with the immediate area of damage.

One thing to remember when approaching repairs to glass fibre hulls is that the average owner is equipped with as much skill as the average workman who originally moulded the boat. As a handyman you can use woodworking and probably metalworking tools. You know something about glues and their uses, you can make joints of sorts. You have some conception of many materials, and how they may be worked in capable hands.

The man who laid up your hull very likely knows nothing but the mechanics of laying up G.R.P. and the Top Ten discs of the week. Remembering the latter may take more brainwork than the former, which is not a skilled job. Under adequate supervision, anyone can lay up G.R.P. Using glass and resin should cause the intelligent handyman no headaches, anyway. The most common damage to G.R.P. hulls is abrasion. Careless handling when coming alongside a quay ; the boat on the next mooring the helmsman on which fails to take into account that the current is stronger than the wind ; a large baulk of timber drifting in the fairway.

Whatever the cause, deep scratches must be repaired at the first possible opportunity—and that means today, preferably, not at laying-up time.

Exposed Fibres

Remember the outside skin of the hull is formed by gel coat, a layer of resin and pigment which may be no more than twenty thousandths of an inch thick. When this is broken, it is almost certain to leave exposed some of the glass fibre ends beneath it—and these can, by capilliary action, draw moisture into the lay up. If this happens, there is very little chance of driving it out again.

Moisture in the lay up is added weight which is not required. But more important, remaining within the skin during the winter, it may freeze, the expansion of water into ice causing serious damage. So, when the hull is scratched deep enough to penetrate the gel coat, no time should be lost in getting it repaired. If the abrasion is wide and shallow, roughen it up well and use the corner of a chisel to make some deeper cuts down into the glass fibres to make the best

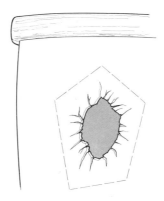

Fig. 8   Where glass fibre is holed, cut right back to pecked line before starting the patch

possible key for a filler. This latter can be resin and pigment mixed—
which can be rather messy to work with. Better is polyester paste of
the sort more commonly used for filling holes in car bodies, and
obtainable from garages and some chandlers. Unfortunately this is
often only obtainable in a rather unpleasant pale green colour, and
will have to be painted over to match the hull. Better is a product
called Plastic Padding Gel Coat, which is made for the very purpose
of filling in abrasions in G.R.P. It is available in several colours.
Whichever product is used, application is very much the same. It is
best to soak the area with resin (mixed with the correct proportion of
catalyst) then smooth the paste on with a knife while the resin is still
wet. Leave it to cure, then rub down with emery cloth.

Serious
Damage

A really severe impact may result in more serious damage. This
could be an area not actually holed, but so fractured that complete
loss of strength takes place. The resin may be pulverized, or at least
broken into a number of small pieces only held together by the fibres
within. There may actually be a hole, this being surrounded by a
further area of strength loss. All the damaged area, in either case,
must be cut out. It is useless to try to patch this up (Fig. 8).

The Method

The tool to use is either a cutting disc on an electric drill, or a
keyhole saw with a metal-cutting blade. When using the first,
caution is necessary; for instance, the type made by a web of very
fine tungsten steel, which is ideal for the job, will take off a finger
even more easily than it will cut G.R.P. It is worth reminding the
reader that there are now high torque electric drills on the market
which operate from a 12-volt car battery, so that this method is not
out of the question even if doing the job afloat.

Once the area is cut out, roughen up the edges of the hole with
the blade of the keyhole saw, to make a keyway. (Make the hole as
geometrical as possible, by the way; it is easier to fill). Clean off all
the resin dust deposited by the cutting, and scrape off paint in a wide
band around the hole, inside the hull, also roughening up the inside
surface within the band as much as possible. Do not clean the hull
surface on the outside of the hull in the vicinity of the hole, but
chamfer the outside edge for about $\frac{1}{8}$ in. all round, leaving it rough.
We want to avoid resin adhering to the outside surface beyond the
chamfer.

Now cut two pieces of woven glass cloth to dimensions about 6 in.
each way larger than the hole. Mix up a small quantity of resin and
catalyst, and paint it thickly all round the hole inside the hull.
Working from the inside, stretch the first piece of cloth over the hole,
rolling it down so that the resin soaks well into the weave. No resin
should be applied to the centre of the cloth at this stage, only to the
border where it overlaps the hull.

Wait until the resin goes tacky, then apply more resin and the
second piece of glass cloth, with the weave of this piece running
diagonally to that of the first piece (Fig. 9). When cutting these two
pieces of glass cloth, allowance should be made for the fact that,

when put on so, at cross purposes, there must still be a good overlap all round. Now wait until the resin has completely hardened.

While waiting, cut four or five pieces of brown paper about the same size as the glass cloth. When ready, mix more resin, and with it soak the whole area of the cloth, including that which masks the hole. Lay on the sheets of brown paper, coating each with resin before the next is applied. This stage has to be completed fairly rapidly, so that all the paper is stuck down and built up to a fair weight before the first coat of resin in the cloth starts to go off.

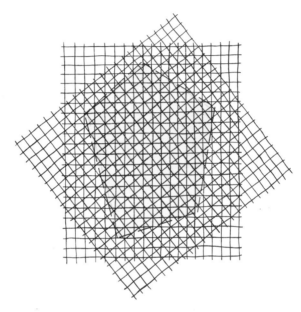

Fig. 9 Diagonally placed glass cloth well outside area which has been cut out

While it is all still wet, mould the whole thickness to the curve of the hull—still working, of course, from the inside. Allow the paper and cloth to set rock hard. The next steps will be made from the outside of the hull, so tools and equipment can be taken up on deck. Seen from the outside, the hole should now appear as a lidless box, as deep as the thickness of the hull, the bottom following the hull's curve. Apply resin liberally to the back and sides of the hole, and insert on top of it a piece of random glass mat cut as near as possible to the correct size and shape. It is possible to spread or compress this slightly, so that it fills all the corners but does not ruck up. Roll it well in so that the resin penetrates the fibre; and although the experts advise against it, I usually soak the mat thoroughly with resin first, then stipple it down with the end of a brush. I have seen too many examples of glass resin lay-up where, on a vertical plane, the resin has not soaked in but merely run down behind the first layer of mat. So that later damage revealed just a bunch of dry glass fibres with no structural strength whatever.

Anyway, make certain that the resin does soak right through, and that no air bubbles remain. Put on more layers of mat to bring the level up to just below the surface of the hull, and allow it to get tacky. Before it cures, the final filling is done either with polyester filler or one of the other preparations mentioned above, allowing this to stand just proud of the outer skin. When that, in turn, hardens off, it can be sanded down.

This type of repair is good for an area up to about two square feet. Anything much larger is really major, of course, probably affecting the structural strength of the hull, and it is then better to get some professional advice on the best method of repair, which will depend on the site of the damage. Painting over the final filling, or adding pigment to it is not, unfortunately, likely to provide such a good colour match that the repair will not be noticeable. It will be necessary to repaint the hull all over if it is required to complete the illusion that no damage has been sustained.

The brown paper, which was built up only as a support for the glass, can quite safely be chipped off and sanded down. If the inside area is hidden by lockers or other panelling, this is not essential. The fairness of the outside line will depend on how much time is expended in emery papering the final filler: wet and dry is the best tool. But if, once this job is commenced, pinholes appear in the filler, gouge it all out down to the glass and re-fill. It will be no use trying to stop the tiny holes—the end result will look like gruyere cheese.

7 Putting off painting it, the use of wax. Tips on paint and painting glass fibre, poor results and good. The use of etching primer, and avoiding damage to the gel coat.

If the hull has suffered damage which has needed repair, it will certainly have to be repainted sooner or later, as colours faded by sun and salt air are almost impossible to match. Even if one is fortunate enough to avoid the normal scrapes and bumps for years, sooner or later repainting will be necessary anyway; for although all the claims made for G.R.P. that it needs no repainting are quite true, they do not tell all the truth.

It is certain that G.R.P. does not have to be repainted, as wood or steel do, in order to preserve it. It does not rot, rust, nor otherwise deteriorate. But we hear a great deal about pollution nowadays, and few people know as much as yachtsmen do about the distressing results pollution of water has been having for years. Try to find a harbour anywhere in Europe, now, where a filthy black oil slick does not stain the waterline. Cross to the Canaries, to the Bahamas, any harbour in the world, in fact, for exactly the same result.

Scrub the hull as often as possible with detergent to keep the worst of this disfigurement away; it will not remove it all, by any means. Polyester resin seems, in time, to take on a permanent stain from oil, and when this stain gets too bad, then it will be time to paint over it for the sake of smartness. Luckily, the original freshness of the gel coat can be retained for a couple of seasons, at least, if the owner is willing to spend time with a tin of polish, such as Johnson's Regatta Wax Polish, and a supply of clean rags.

The ideal thing is to start from new, of course; but even if the boat has just this minute been delivered, it will need a thorough wash down with warm water and a mild detergent such as washing-up liquid. The glass fibre reinforced plastic comes greasy from the mould; builders' hands will have been all over it, leaving more grubby marks; and to these layers will adhere a patina of dust and chemicals from the atmosphere. Minute though the quantities may be, there is no point in sealing them down on to the polyester in order to continue chemical reaction at their leisure.

Wash the yacht down from coach roof to boot topping, then. Use soft cloths, but rub vigorously to make certain that it really is clean. It is best to do this on a sunny day, of course, when the surface will dry off quickly. But as it is unwise to waste too much time after delivery, a calm day will do even if not too warm, and on the whole it is better to have a slightly damp atmosphere than a dry dusty one.

Applying Polish

If the boat is not new, there is obviously not the same urgency— but the sooner done the better. In years to come there may probably be a set of statistics showing how many more years a G.R.P. hull, polished, lasts compared with an unpolished one. All we know at the moment is that wax protects.

Until anyone has actually applied a coat of wax polish to even the hull of a dinghy, he cannot realize just what sort of task he has set himself. On a cruiser the hull, the cockpit and cabin top combined, total up a quite fantastic square footage. But it is a labour much more than just worth while, for it is at least putting off the time when the hull will have to be repainted.

It is important to use a good plain wax polish for this job. Avoid products with silicones or other additives, as some of these substances have an adverse effect on G.R.P. Some of the chief polish manufacturers now sell products especially designed for glass fibre boats, and it is unlikely that there is anything more suitable. Of course, one waxing will not last a boat a lifetime, any more than it will a car. The more often it is done, the easier the job and the better the protection. It is certainly a good idea to give one coat at the beginning, and a final one at the end of each season—the latter to help it through the winter; then a good wash down in the spring and start again with the wax. However lovingly the boat is waxed, however, the time will inevitably come when paint is necessary; as far as G.R.P. is concerned, that point is personal to each owner. When he can no longer bear to sail in such a scruffy looking yacht, that is the time.

First Principles

Painting a glass fibre boat is very much like painting any other sort of boat—or even like painting a house. There are important differences, which I shall explain. But first, for those many people (such as Council House tenants), who until they became boat owners would have considered it beneath their dignity to touch a paint brush, I offer some advice on applying paint generally.

I am not advising the more knowledgeable to turn away until the ignorant have finished reading this bit; for there never yet was anyone who knew all there is to know about this—or any—subject, and I am reasonably confident that there will be one or two tips here which even old hands will not have heard. After 20 years of painting boats, I am constantly discovering that there are new ways of cutting corners. I remember, even when I was a boy, that my father made the accidental discovery that a certain brand of disinfectant, sold for cleaning w.c. bowls, was unbeatable for cleaning paint brushes. Even weeks old paint hardened in the bristles would melt away before it. He wrote to the manufacturers and told them, expecting to be handsomely rewarded, and they did in fact send him a free bottle of the stuff. It was some years before they actually mentioned this attribute of their product in their sales literature, however. It is not even made any more, as far as I know. And today there are purpose-made products which do an equally good job. Most are much more expensive, naturally.

Anyway, the following remarks are intended to pass on some general tips about painting, and call attention to some common faults which, unless they be recognized, will almost certainly mean a result less than perfect. They apply, in most cases, to boats of whatever the hull material.

(a) If, when a new tin of paint is opened, it proves to have a skin on the surface, take it back to the shop. If this is impractical, or if it is not a new tin, remove the skin carefully and whole, and throw it away.

Never stir it in, hoping for the best. It will *not* mix with the paint. What it will do is break up into thousands of small pieces which cling to the brush every time it is dipped, and impart to the hull a pebble-dashed appearance. If the skin has been stirred in there are two remedies. Throw it all away and buy a new tin, or strain through muslin. The former is easier and less messy. How can you prevent skin forming in the first place? Ignore old-timers who urge that half-empty tins should be stored upside down. The skin will still form on the top surface—it is air which causes it—and you have merely stored up trouble, as the top becomes the bottom when the tin is turned right way up for opening. Now the skin is hidden below the surface, and when stirred merely breaks up on the bottom instead of the top. The result is the same.

The best way to prevent skin forming is to pour about an eggcupful of white spirit or turpentine on top of the paint before closing the lid, if it will be more than 24 hours before using it again. Do not stir it in or shake the tin, which should be stored right way up until next wanted.

(b) Sometimes, as paint or varnish is applied, the surface of the painted article starts to look like orange peel—covered with craters and bumps. The more attempts made to brush this out, the worse the effect becomes. On a G.R.P. hull this is almost certainly caused by grease, wax, dust or silicones—or possibly by a thin layer of moisture, perhaps condensing itself on to the surface as fast as attempts are made to dry it. On a wooden hull, it would probably be caused by the timber being damp. The only cure is to clean the new paint right off again before it dries (it will *not* improve as it dries), using white spirit or turps. If dampness of the atmosphere is judged to be the cause, it is useless to start again until conditions improve.

(c) Blisters may form on the surface as the paint dries. This is more usual with wooden hulls, and is caused usually by moisture in the wood evaporating, the vapour becoming trapped between hull and paint skin. It can also happen with G.R.P. if the gel coat surface has crazed and moisture lies in the hairline cracks. If there is any sign of crazing, it is important to paint on a dry, warm day. When painting wooden or metal parts of the hull, blisters may also form, caused by resinous knots or corrosion. Knots should always be treated with knotting, which forms an impervious skin, before painting, and corroded metal with one of the correct corrosion inhibitors for the particular metal. Once blisters form, there is no way of repairing them. By that time the paint skin is practically dry, and getting it all off again will be a man-sized job. Prevention by correct preparation is the only answer.

(d) If the gloss has a dull sheen, instead of a bright one, this is probably due to painting in unsuitable weather. Fine rain or frost can be responsible, or an atmosphere laden with dew. It may also be caused by atmospheric pollution; sulphur from factory chimneys can travel long distances before settling, so don't discount this because there are no factories near. Try not to paint when there is a wind blowing from the direction in which lies an industrial area within twenty miles or so.

(e) Poor results are often blamed on poor preparation, with justice. Wood grain not properly sanded, undercoat applied too thinly and then not rubbed down sufficiently. The very best gloss paint is only as good as the surface to which it is applied; it can have a finish like limewash if proper preparation tactics are ignored.

Tricks of the Trade

When it comes to painting a yacht, owners tend to think that some of the easy methods they do not scruple to use when 'doing' the children's bedroom, are not suitable for the pride of their lives. In fact, many of the tricks of the home handyman can make life very much easier. There is absolutely no reason, for example, why the ubiquitous paint roller should not be used for applying undercoat to the hull. It is much quicker, and puts on a slightly thinner coat than does a brush.

It is best, however, to put the first undercoat on with a brush, as the action of brushing helps to emulsify any slight film of grease which may have escaped the preliminary wash down. But another two coats can be put on very quickly with a roller. Sand each coat as soon as dry and before applying the next, naturally; then put the final undercoat on with a brush. The first very much thinned top coat—and do use proper thinners, not white spirit—can go on with a roller. But after that use a clean new brush for the enamel.

Taking Trouble

It is worth saying here—and it applies to everything to do with boats—that trouble taken repays a thousandfold. Not so long ago I was strolling through a busy marina on the south coast. It was June, and most yachts were in the water; only a few were still ashore. One oldish sailing craft, perched on its cradle, was nearing the point when the owner would send for the Travelift. He was standing in the cockpit, paintbrush in hand, looking about for what more he could touch up. What absolutely staggered me was the perfection of his varnished brightwork; it was like a mirror, and without the slightest speck of dust or other blemish. Naturally I stopped to admire, and asked him what varnish he had used. He named a well-known and not particularly expensive brand, one which I had used with quite good results, but nothing approaching those he had obtained. However, as he did not seem inclined to talk, I strolled on.

Returning some time later I found the cockpit inhabited by the man's wife—he was not to be seen—and obviously recognizing me as the nosey parker, she smiled. Encouraged, I stopped to ask *her* how he had got such wonderful results. She raised her eyes in the manner women usually employ to indicate long suffering. 'Time', she said. 'If you only knew how much time'.

It turned out that he was one of those characters for whom nothing is too much trouble. In the first place, he would not lift a paint brush unless the weather was absolutely right for humidity, temperature and wind—the latter he would have none of. He left each coat for at least a week, then spent another week sanding it down before standing by to wait for the perfect weather conditions necessary before applying the next coat. And so on. Most of his sailing was done each year in August and September—he seldom managed to get afloat in time for July. The point of the story is that, if enough trouble is taken, superb results can be obtained by anyone. Few of us will take that amount of pains; but we should set ourselves a limit below which we refuse to drop. Knowing that we can, if we feel like it, reach the same state of perfection as the man in the marina. This applies not only to varnishing, of course, but also to painting, outside and in.

Etching Primer

Ten years or so ago there was no satisfactory way of painting a G.R.P. hull. The Royal Navy tried all manner of experiments and failed to find a solution; and they came within an ace of giving up G.R.P. boats because of it. The material is so slick that no paint, not even the polyurethanes, will stick to it; and the high speeds used by naval craft caused paint to peel off like onion skin.

Fortunately, within the last few years, the efforts of paint manufacturers have met with success; and they have rediscovered the method long used for making paint stick to steel hulls. Etching primer.

This is a very thin liquid with an acid base, and is painted on to the hull with an ordinary paint brush. Its action is to roughen the outer surface, the gel coat, sufficiently to form a key. And very effective it is, too. It softens the resin for a short period, then dries again, leaving the etched surface. The hull is then washed off and, when dry, is ready to receive the paint. Using etching primer on G.R.P. is, in fact, a much quicker process than stripping down, sanding, priming and painting a wooden hull. Many people recommend that a polyurethane paint should be used on G.R.P., and this seems logical. Plastic paint to plastic hull. But my personal preference is for the traditional type of yacht enamel, which goes on to fibre glass equally well.

I painted my hull for the first time two winters ago. After the etching primer I used two undercoats and two top coats of a well known make of ordinary marine enamel. The paint is unbroken, no cracks or chips. It has the inevitable oil stains and will have to be done next winter again, for appearance sake. Unfortunately I shall have to strip off the last coat before putting the new one on. No top

coat of paint should be left uncovered by a new coat of paint for
more than twelve months. Any time longer than a year, and it should
be stripped, as it gets too brittle, and the surface too impervious to
take a satisfactory key. Unfortunately, etching primer cannot be used
to etch paint; so we have to go back to standard procedure—sand all
over. Paint strippers definitely must not be used, and even sand paper
must be used with care so that the gel coat is not damaged.
Blowlamps—absolutely out—never, never on a G.R.P. hull. For one
thing, the resin is inflammable unless a fire retarding chemical has
been included in the lay-up, and this is unlikely because of expense.
And even if such care could be used that the boat did not catch fire,
the heat would certainly damage the gel coat.

8

Simple beginning, a binocular box, stowage nets for deckhead, under bunk spaces and the side decks. Bosun's stores, how to supply and fit stowage racks to cockpit lockers to which there is minimum access.

Everything which has gone before, so far, is to help make additions to a G.R.P. yacht—additions which will improve her, make her more convenient, and so easier to handle. And because, being a small glass fibre craft she is almost certainly a production job, to give her some of the individuality which she otherwise lacks. As already made clear, the work ahead inevitably means that the owner must become a ship's carpenter; and with the information already available, this is not too frightening a prospect. But for the sake of practice with basic tools, it is a good idea to start with something simple—a binocular box, for example.

A binocular box is virtually a necessity on every cruising boat, but it is seldom that one is seen on smaller craft. Screwed to a panel just inside the cabin, such a box ensures that the glasses are always to hand when wanted by whoever is on watch; there is no struggle to get them out of a leather case in a hurry; nor are they in danger of damage as they are when slung permanently around the helmsman's neck.

So far as I know, it is not possible to go into a shop and buy the sort of box I mean. This is probably because there are so many different makes and sizes of binoculars, and one 'standard-sized' box would be of no use to most. It is important that the glasses be a snug but comfortable fit in their container. Working with $\frac{3}{16}$ in. plywood, dovetailing would be a tricky, if not impossible operation, and there is no point in attempting it. I made my box from marine plywood—though in fact it does not need to be of marine grade for this job. The box will not get wet unless the boat sinks, and a pair of 7 × 50 glasses will not be of much worry then, anyway. An offcut of oak-faced interior grade is cheaper, and gives the box an excellent appearance.

This is for the sides. The bottom is made from a piece of solid wood $\frac{1}{2}$ in. thick. Deal, pine, or any type of wood will do, as it will never be seen (Fig. 10). Glue and pin (using copper covered panel pins) the four sides to this base, then join each corner vertically with a length of $\frac{3}{8}$ in. triangular ash beading. This is also glued and pinned from the outside. Use very fine wire pins for this; these are not driven right home, for fear of splitting the beading. Once the glue has set they are removed and a little sawdust and glue rubbed into the holes.

The base of the box is made $\frac{1}{2}$ in. longer and wider than the dimensions of the binoculars when they are extended to their widest on the centre pivot. Or, if only one person is likely to use them (a single handed sailor!) $\frac{1}{2}$ in. greater than the dimensions when the glasses are adjusted to that person's eyes. They will then always come from the box at the correct extension.

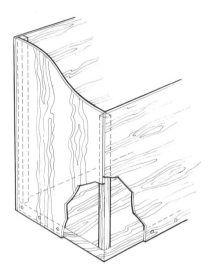

Fig. 10   Part of binocular box

The back is made to the height of the glasses at their fullest telescopic extension, plus $\frac{1}{2}$ in. for the base. And the front is $1\frac{1}{2}$ in. shorter than the back. The sides can be cut off at an angle, or shaped in a double or reverse curve, which can be cut with a fretsaw, keyhole saw, or shaped with an American spokeshave. Clamp both ends together while cutting, so that they are identical.

My box is fixed so that it is covered by the sliding hatchway when the latter is fully closed, and is fastened to a G.R.P. panel which forms the side of a locker there. I was therefore able to through-bolt, with bearing pad behind the panel. I drilled two holes through the back of the box, an inch from the top edge and about an inch from each side. I countersank these on the inside of the box, to take cheese headed bolts ($\frac{1}{4}$ in. diameter, $\frac{3}{4}$ in. long are large enough) and then marked their position on the G.R.P. panel and drilled through that.

The inside of the box was then lined with green polyurethane foam—the colour is unimportant—which makes a better padding than baize. It is also slightly thicker—I used $\frac{1}{4}$ in. thick sheet foam, which just took up the extra $\frac{1}{2}$ in. I had allowed in the dimensions, with plenty of 'give'. I also used it because small sheets still cost only a few coppers in Woolworth's. A rubber-based glue is used to attach the foam to the inside of the box, cutting out each area separately. There is no need to cut holes in it for the bolts, because they push through without any trouble, and are then hidden by the foam. If ply faced with hardwood has been used, the box only needs sanding and varnishing. If it is faced with birch, then it will be better painted. My box has now been in use for three seasons; I must admit that I was doubtful about its strength for the position it was in, at first; but it has taken plenty of knocks as clumsy sailors go below through the small hatchway, and is still as solid as ever.

Stowage Nets   The captain of an ocean-going liner probably has difficulty in finding sufficient stowage space for all his dunnage. The problems of owner and crew of a 20 ft. pleasure craft are even more acute. The ubiquitous kitbag is usually called in to deal with that of clothes; but what about charts, and flags, and distress flares, and navigational equipment; almanacs, foghorns, cordage, sail repairing equipment, riding lights, spare shackles . . . ? A book published in the early 1920's, discussing the husbandry of 'small cruising yachts', devoted about eight pages to lists of the essentials, and recommended that all

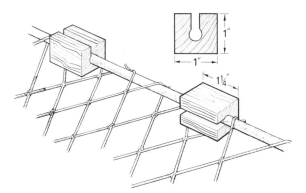

Fig. 11

these items should be stowed in their own bins, or canvas bags, in the fo'c'sle. Half of those items would sink today's 'small yacht'. But it is, of course, absolutely essential to make arrangements for stowing necessary items in such a manner that they can be found immediately when wanted.

On a wooden boat it is, for example, a simple matter to rig nets across the deckhead, fastening to the beams through plywood discs. The space between the beams then makes an ideal and handy place for charts, signal flags, the ensign and the skipper's spare socks. There is little if any loss of headroom. On a glass fibre boat, however, there are few supporting frames—often none—and in any case they will not take screws. With the use of Rawlnuts it would be possible to attach nets to the deckhead liner, if any. But in the small G.R.P. cruiser headroom is already at a premium, and the loss of another few inches would be insupportable.

On my own sloop I needed nets in several places. Under the bunks are spaces—they cannot be called lockers—into which the only access is from above, through lift-off plywood covers. Below are the concavities of the bilge keels, which get nastily wet from condensation; because I have taken steps to prevent this in the cabin, it all seems to happen down below. It is therefore impossible to keep clothes, or anything else which can be spoiled by moisture, down there, unless nets are rigged to keep gear clear of the bottom and sides of the hull. I also wanted nets under the side decks throughout the cabin, so that the occupants of the four bunks have somewhere to stow *their* socks, instead of leaving them all over the cabin sole. The main problem in rigging these nets was that a number of attachment points were needed—some in places where I could bolt through, which seemed a clumsy way of fixing a net; somewhere resin and glass tape could be used, also clumsy.

After some thought, I solved the problem by using my power saw at home to cut a large number of hardwood blocks. I used teak because I happened to have some strips of 1 in. square section teak handy; but any other hardwood would do, except mahogany. Mahogany often chips easily, and it must be possible to cut with the grain to make these blocks, as well as across it. I cut the wood into pieces $1\frac{1}{4}$ in. long, so that I had blocks $1\frac{1}{4} \times 1 \times 1$ in. This is quite an arbitrary measurement—but if they were much smaller it would be difficult to carry out the remainder of the necessary work on them. While if larger they would not only be clumsy, but it might be necessary to shape one side to the curve of the hull. (Fig. 11)

Through each block I drilled a hole $\frac{1}{4}$ in. diameter, lengthways with the grain (through the longest measurement). Then, along one of the sides of each block I cut a slot downwards until it met the hole. This slot was slightly less in thickness than the diameter of the hole, and I found a keyhole saw the best tool for the job. A few of the blocks were simply drilled, but no slot cut.

The blocks then were glued to the hull, bulkheads, etc., on a level where the net was to be hung. Where access to the net was to be from above—as under the bunk spaces—they were glued all round the perimeter at 18 in. spaces. Along the side of the hull, that is, on bulkheads at each end of the space, and along the vertical inboard panel. They were set and glued so that the slot was on the upper surface of each block, running parallel with the side to which it was fastened.

Under the side decks I spaced them 18 in. apart along the hull,
but only every 3 ft on the inboard side, where access to the net was
to be sideways between the deckhead and edge of the net. The
blocks were glued in place with epoxy resin glue. Each position was
first marked with a pencil, then the area scraped for removal of paint,
roughened and degreased, as already described. The main difficulty
was to keep slight but adequate pressure on the blocks while the
glue cured, and this involved using a spiderweb of thin battens.
These were used to hold two or three blocks on one length where
they came on the same level, with other short lengths acting as props
against the nearest solid footing.

A strong, cheap and quite suitable netting to use is polythene
garden netting, supplied by most ironmongers and garden centres.
The meshes are all welded, so there is no danger of runs when it is
cut; and a 50p. packet contains enough net to camouflage a
Centurion tank. Cut it into pieces of the sizes needed; two people are
needed for this job, for unless it is held taut while being cut, all
sense of direction is soon lost, and the result is a most peculiar shape.
Lengths of thin shockcord are cut to such a length so that, when
joined end to end (whipped together), they have a slightly smaller
circumference than those of the rings of blocks to which they are to
be attached. Before whipping together the ends of the shockcord,
thread it through the outside meshes of the net. When the ends are
joined, stretch the cord and push it down into the slots cut in the
blocks. The net should now be taut over its whole area; but if it sags
anywhere, take a loop of codline through a mesh in the slack area,
and draw it towards the shockcord.

On the deckhead, the slots need to be facing downwards, and it is
better to have blocks with holes but no slots positioned against the
hull. Otherwise the cord may slip out in a place where it is difficult to
reach to replace. This means threading each 18 in. of net with the
cord, passing the end through a block, then threading the next
length of net, and so on. A tedious job, but secure once finished.

If desired to save shockcord—which can be bought by the yard
from chandlers in various thicknesses, to suit the diameter of the
holes in the blocks—codline can be used around three quarters of the
net's circumference, whipping in only a short length of shockcord to
give the required stretch. It is, of course, not absolutely necessary to
cut slots in any of the blocks. But they do make rigging easier; and
are also useful in underbunk spaces, where the net can be unhooked
from one or two of the blocks when it is necessary to get to the
bottom of the bilge. This allows heavy gear, such as a spare anchor,
to be stowed underneath the net.

Having used garden netting, it is easy to make the whole thing
look more seamanlike at very little cost. I found, for example, that the
netting under the side decks presented a rather untidy appearance,
with cut edges sticking out into the cabin. To cure this I bought a
couple of yards of small mesh string netting, about 18 in. wide. This
I cut into 2-in. strips, smeared one side of each strip with clear
rubber solution, and folded it in place over the shockcord and

inboard edge of the garden netting. Pressed together, the folded white net stuck to itself through the wider mesh of the garden net, and a clean neat edge is now presented to the cabin. The tackiness of the rubber solution wore off after a few hours.

Bo'sun's Stores

As a rest from the simple if laborious task of cutting slots in small blocks of wood, we now move on to a rougher job—rougher, but one which can provide, in miniature, an approximation to the bo'sun's store taken for granted in all 'small cruising yachts' by the out-of-date author I mentioned just now.

It is a belief common to nearly every designer of small glass fibre boats that adequate strength can only be obtained by totally enclosing 85 per cent of the hull's cubic capacity. Because cruising yachtsmen insist on living in and storing things within the hull, the smallest possible holes are cut to give access where absolutely essential. They are usually holes made as difficult as possible to get at, too—as under the bunk cushions. We should like to see a designer trying to move a mattress (preferably with the man just off watch sleeping on it), in a Force 7 in the Channel—perhaps looking for the sea anchor. Because of this idiosyncrasy, most small yachts have two lockers in the cockpit, the interiors of which are reached through lifting wooden lids. Lids which are often half as long and half as wide as the lockers they cover. The result of this is that nothing can be arranged within them, because it is as much as one can do to get an arm in, let alone arrange racks, bins and calico bags for the neat stowage recommended (Fig. 12).

The warps, fenders, buckets, etc., normally kept in the cockpit lockers are consequently always in a tangle, and this is not only unseamanlike, it can be dangerous when warp or fender is needed in a hurry. Even a small cubical space is of more use if it can be divided up in some way, and lockers of this sort need racks, so that different items can be stowed at different levels. If we build a rack to fit the space, however, (and it must fit tightly if it is not just to become part of the jumble—it will not pass through the lid. There is, of course, no possibility of building the rack *in situ*.

The only possibility in such cases is to make a rack in collapsible parts. I made one for each of my two cockpit lockers. In the starboard one, which formerly held only the gas bottle and fuel tank for the auxiliary outboard, I now have a rack which fills that half of the locker above which there is no access. The fuel tank stands on this, and a shallow bin slides in and out underneath it, in which is kept paint and varnish, turps, glues, mastic, freeing oil, etc., etc. All immediately to hand when wanted, but usually out of the way in a space previously unusable. In that locker there is now room for, besides gas bottle and fuel tank, two gallon cans of petrol, one can of paraffin, the storm lantern, anchor buoy—and a small Seagull outboard for the dinghy.

In the port locker (access to which is so minute that it is a squeeze to get a polythene bucket through) the rack holds fenders and nothing else. Under it go my seaboots, and the bucket stands immediately below the lid. There is also a row of pegs on which hang coiled warps.

The racks are made in two parts. The spaces in which they have to fit are very unsymmetrical, being positioned on the yacht's quarters.

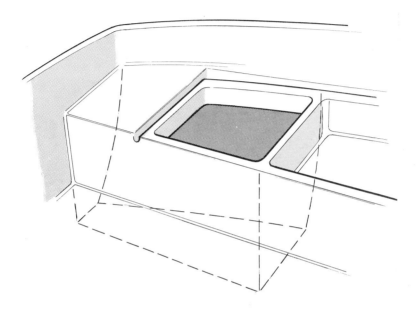

Fig. 12   Typical cockpit locker with small access and of irregular shape

Dimensions on the floor of the lockers are therefore different to the dimensions at the top of the locker space, and it is of course necessary to measure all the different dimensions reasonably accurately if the racks are to be of any use. The easiest way to get accurate measurements in such a space is to use two pieces of batten, each of them shorter than the measurement to be made, but greater than it when combined. Held firmly in the fist, they can be extended until their opposite ends touch the sides of the space; then, gripped tightly, they are withdrawn and the length measured from tip to tip. This rack was made for the port locker, the cockpit seat opening above the fore end of the space, which runs back to- wards the stern right up to the transom. The outer—or hull—side of the locker is naturally curved two ways, while the inboard side is a vertical plane. The principle described here may, of course, be applied to lockers of any shape or size, with top or side openings, where access is too limited for any other means to be used.

Top widths A–B and C–D must be measured at the correct height (Fig. 13). This is extremely important for A–B, which fortunately is the most accessible, not quite so important for C–D. Make the latter measurement too small rather than too large. The two parts to be

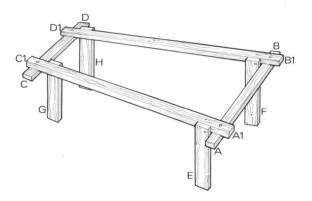

Fig. 13

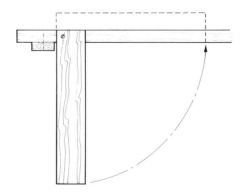

Fig. 14   Positioning the legs to assist folding

made are the frame and the table. Main dimensions for the frame are those on floor level, E–F and G–H, the latter, in the stern, being narrower than the former. E–G and F–H will give the length of the rack, and are important because the irregular shape of the space makes width and length interdependent if the rack is to be a snug fit.

Make the uprights of $1\frac{1}{2} \times 1$ in. timber, about half the height of the locker, allowing for the fact that the level of the table will be $1\frac{1}{2}$ in. above the height of these uprights. Measure width of locker A–B and cut crosspieces of $1\frac{1}{2} \times \frac{1}{2}$ in. wood to this length. Put this in position in the locker and hold upright F under it vertically, with its foot at the point where hull and floor meet. Mark on A–B where top of the upright comes.

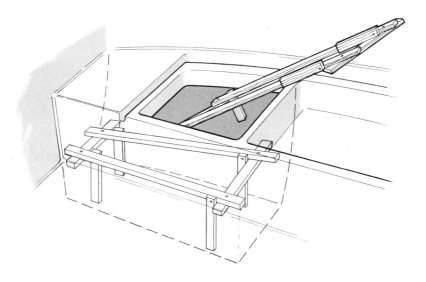

Fig. 15   Passing the frame into the locker

The longitudinal D¹–B¹ must not fall outside this mark. And the top of each leg must just meet the top side of the longitudinals. I found it impossible to get to the back of the locker to make an accurate measurement of crosspiece C–D, and I did it by guess and trial and error. It is better to be too narrow than too wide in such an inaccessible place. Height, of course, is the same at both ends. Now working outside the locker, in the open, join the two crosspieces

together with longitudinals from A–C and B–D. A^1–C^1 is positioned
$1\frac{1}{2}$ in. from the bulkhead, and is screwed into AB and CD with a
single 1 in. screw in each position.

The legs are now screwed to C^1, A^1, D^1 and B^1. Drill the screw-

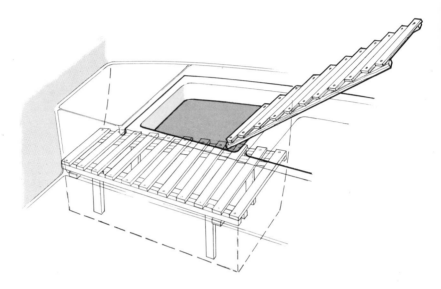

Fig. 16

holes in the uprights at A and B off centre, so that when the legs are
folded up their bottom edges are flush with the bottom edges of the
longitudinals A^1–C^1 and B^1–D^1. The legs are positioned as shown
in Fig. 14—important, to facilitate folding. The uprights at C and
D do not need to be folded up, as they go into the locker first and
without difficulty.

Because of the method of construction, the frame can now be
pressed into a parallelogram until it is narrow enough to pass
through the locker opening with the forward legs folded up. (Fig. 15)
Once down into the space, it is pulled open again to make a snug fit,
and the legs lowered. If it has been made to the correct dimensions
the legs will all touch the floor of the locker, while crosspieces A–B
and C–D fit snugly against the sides and are partly supported by the
inward curve of the hull. The apparent flimsiness of the fastenings is
immaterial, because the structure should now be held together by the
shape of the locker.

The table consists of a number of thin slats screwed across two
heavier longitudinals with a single screw at each join. The slats will

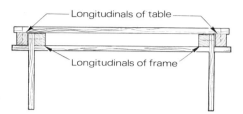

Longitudinals of table

Longitudinals of frame

Fig. 17

get progressively longer from aft in this particular locker (Fig. 16), but perfect fit of the slats between bulkhead and hull is not necessary. The important measurement is that between the longitudinals, which should drop just outside the longitudinals of the frame (Fig. 17). Remember that there is only $1\frac{1}{2}$ in. of space between frame A–C and the side of the locker.

The slats should be spaced about 2 in. apart—more or less according to the size of the opening through which the table has to be pushed. The wider apart they are, the narrower it will fold (Fig. 16). Concertina it, put it into the locker, open it out and drop it into place. I found no need to join the table to the frame—again, the shape of the space makes the whole thing solid. But different shaped lockers will have other problems, and it might in some cases be necessary to bolt the table to the frame. This will best be done through the longitudinals. It might also, in some cases, be necessary to make the table in two halves, in order to get it through the locker opening and over the frame.

Making and Fixing Pegs

The rack in this locker was situated aft, and the space immediately under the lifting lid left clear and to full depth. It was in this space that I rigged pegs to hold warps. This was done by taking a piece of 3×2 in. timber 30 in. long (which was all the space I had) and drilling four equally spaced $\frac{1}{2}$ in. holes through it, all at an angle of $45°$, so that the pegs would project upwards at that angle when the strip was fastened horizontally. Into each hole I glued a 6 in. length of $\frac{1}{2}$ in. ash dowel, which left 4 in. protruding. A 1 in. disc of plywood was screwed to the outer end of each peg.

The back of the 3×2 in. was slightly curved to follow the shape of the hull, and the rack glued on as high as it would go and still allow a couple of lengths of rope to slip over the end of each peg. The glueing was done with the care already described, using epoxy glue, and the rack supported in position for a week while the glue set.

9 Small but important improvements to the accommodation. Need for stowage in the galley. How to keep the cans in order and a method of stowing the china. Making sure the pans stay on a non-gimballed stove, and a bookcase where there was none.

With the determination, as a selling point, to cram at least four berths into a 21 footer, and more recently five berths into 22 footers, the designer of the small G.R.P. cruising yacht has little space in which to provide gracious living afloat. In my own sloop, for example, the galley is reasonable as far as it goes. There is a two-burner and grill Calor gas stove, and a sink, set side by side in a console which extends out to the gangway line. Beneath this is a locker, extending over the whole area of the console, but only a foot high. Two drop doors give access to it, but to see what is in it, my face has to be resting on the cabin sole.

Behind the console are two G.R.P. bins large enough to hold a couple of bottles of milk, butter, and anything else which needs keeping cool. There is no drain to them, so they are not intended as ice boxes. But they do provide a reasonably low temperature. There is nothing to complain at in this arrangement, the total storage space for food being sufficient for the sort of cruising most likely in a yacht of this size. But improvements could be made—and the most important is the provision of a method of getting cans out of the locker below.

For not only is it impossible to see what is in that locker unless one is a contortionist; but also, because the locker is one overall space, everything stowed in it, however neatly, gets hopelessly jumbled up in any sort of seaway. Nor are the drop doors adequate for stemming a rush of heavy cans; a sudden lurch can deposit all the contents of the locker on the cabin sole. Another improvement is to devise some sort of rack in which to store crockery. No thought whatever was given to this problem by the designer. He gave us not even space to stow a cup; and as one cannot even put cuphooks into G.R.P., these important utensils usually ended up tucked under bunk cushions.

Drawer Space Sorting out the food locker was fairly simple. It merely meant making two boxes of such dimensions that they would fill the space in the lockers, yet pull out through the drop doors. They were made of ¾ in. white wood, the sides dovetailed into front and back to prevent any chance of separation when they were pulled out while containing a fair weight. The bottom of each drawer was made of

¼ in. birch plywood, which was grooved into the four sides to prevent weight pushing it out. As the boxes, or drawers, were hidden in the ordinary way by the drop doors, there seemed no point in facing them with mahogany ply. They were, therefore, merely coloured with mahogany stain and varnished. Each was provided with a rope handle, and the interiors were divided up with partitions, further to prevent tins from sliding about. (Fig. 18) The partitions,

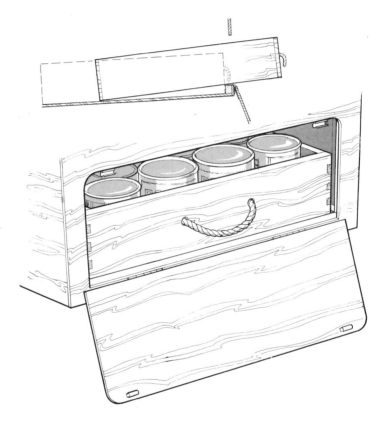

Fig. 18

grooved into the sides and screwed and glued to the bottom panels, also gave the drawers added strength. An arc had to be cut from the back of the one which slid under the sink, in order to prevent its snagging on the plastic waste pipe. Fortunately, the drop doors were hinged to battens which made stops over which the drawers have to be lifted. If they had not been there, I should have provided stops, in order to prevent the weight coming against the doors themselves. When deciding the height of the drawers, the thickness of the batten must be taken into consideration. As I said, this was a fairly simple solution to a problem. The one of stowage for crockery was more difficult. One of my early provisions for cups was to bolt a strip of wood behind the G.R.P. lip formed where the coachroof meets the side deck moulding, and to screw cup hooks up into this wood. This was a temporary solution as the cups could not be expected to remain on hooks when the boat was sailing.

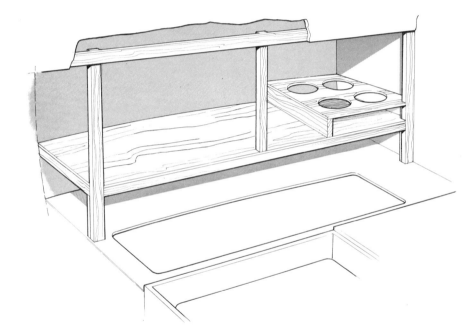

Fig. 19

A Plate Rack   While we pigged it with enamel plates (with signal flags printed on them!) and mugs, it did not really matter that these were stowed under bunks, though they crashed about rather in a seaway, and were a nuisance to fish out of the bilge. But when the case for more gracious living afloat was urged, this just would not do, so I got down to designing a plate rack. The length of wood holding the cuphooks was removed, and for it was substituted a piece of 1 in. × ½ in. section, the same length as the galley console. The width of the

side deck is about 14 in., and the height from the lift off wooden lids
covering the cool lockers behind the galley, to the side deck, is also
about 14 in. I intended to put my plate rack into this space, while
still leaving access to the cool lockers.

Before bolting into position, behind the G.R.P. lip, the length of
1 in. × ½ in. (with the long face vertical, as it has to be drawn into
the curve of the deck), I half-jointed on to it three lengths of 1 × ½ in.
wood to make vertical supports—two of them dropping from the top
horizontal to the galley level. These were one at each end, of course,
positioned so that they did not interfere with the lids of the cool bins.
The third was only 7 in. long, giving an actual drop from the bottom
of the G.R.P. lip of 6 in. (Fig. 19). Now, at the level 6 in. below the
lip, I traced out the shape of the area bounded on one side by the
slightly curved hull, and on the other by a line dropped from the lip
and following its curve. To this pattern I cut a piece of ⅜ in. plywood,
for a bottom. A length of ½ in. square softwood was screwed and
glued to the inboard top edge of this, forcing it into the slight curve.
The three 1 × ½ in. drops were half jointed into this.
I was able to screw both my end vertical drops into bulkheads. Had
this not been possible, I should have devised a method for holding
their bottom ends, such as wooden U-pieces glued down to the
galley top. The centre vertical was not positioned—and its half
joints not made—until I had decided on the sizes of plates I intended
to stow in the rack. It had to fall between the arcs made by two
piles of plates.

The top rail, as when used just for cuphooks, was bolted through
the G.R.P. lip, and the shaped plywood bottom now had its inboard
edge held firmly in place by the three verticals. The outboard
edge, though not supported by frames, was firmly held to a horizontal
position by the inward curve of the hull.

The front of the rack is most important, and its shape must be
decided on with care. It depends again on what sort of plates, and
what sizes are to be stored in it. A piece of mahogany faced plywood
as long as the rack and 3 in. wide (4 in. if soup plates are to be
included, or if it is intended to stow more than four plates in each
slot) is marked off along one edge with centres for the plates. For
example, suppose that it is intended to stow 10 in. dinner plates,
9 in. soup plates, and 7 in. side plates. Mark a point 5 in. from one
end, then measure another 5 in. plus ½ in. for space between, then
mark a centre at 4½ in. Measure another 4½ in. plus ½ in. for space
between, then a centre at 3½ in.

Now, in the three centres marked, cut steep-sided waves, or 'U'-
shaped slots, 3 in. wide (Fig. 20). Allow for the height of the lip of
each type of plate, so that the lip will project through the 'U' when
the plate is sitting firmly on the bottom of the rack. This front, or
'cover', is screwed and glued on to the framework already in place.
The plates have to be put in over the top of the cover and dropped
down into position so that an arc protrudes. Many more expensive
boats provide a plate rack something like this—but usually with only
a very narrow front slot, so that the plates have to be dropped down

into position from a great height, I like better the idea of having a good large arc of crockery to grasp.

Where such racks are provided by builders, however, nothing is usually done to allow for plates of different sizes. The front of the rack is parallel with the hull; and if a 10 in. plate is firmly gripped between front and hull, the 7 in. one is able to crash about with 3 in. liberty. This can be overcome as the builders do it, by providing partitions between each section, so that the crashing can only be done athwartships. Or it can be done, more simply and effectively by providing a spring, designed to grip the plates between the hull side and the front cover of the rack.

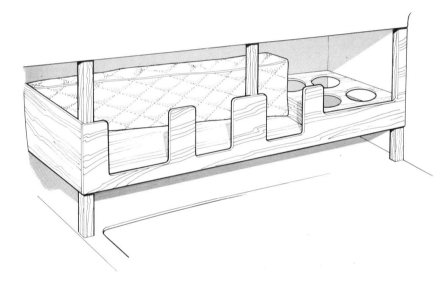

Fig. 20   Plate and mug positions. Sponge rubber against side of boat

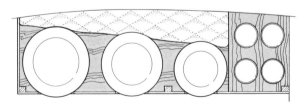

Fig. 21

My spring consisted of a slab of soft plastic foam, 2 in. thick, 6 in. wide and as long as the rack. I cut this through its thickness so that it tapered off from its full thickness (behind the smallest plates) to about $\frac{1}{2}$ in. (behind the largest). This is easily glued in place against the side of the hull with a rubber glue, once the G.R.P. surface has been degreased. Cutting plastic foam is liable to be a fairly rough job, but this does not matter; the rough side can be glued, leaving the smooth side outwards to the rack. Finally, cut to size a piece of spongeable vinyl material, such as quilted plastic, and glue this on top of the foam plastic. Now each plate, as it goes into the rack, has to be pressed back against the sponge and down into its space. It cannot move until the human hand pushes and lifts. (Fig. 21)

In making the plate rack, it then seemed right to provide proper stowage for cups. With the three sizes of plate, there was still space of about 10 in. left on the plate rack level. I therefore made a plywood 'table', on 2 in. legs, of a size to fit tightly between the hull and the

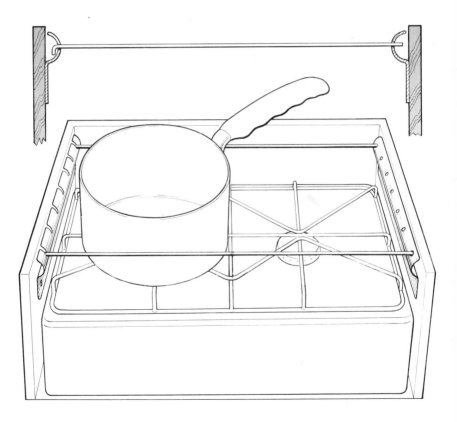

Fig. 22

front of the rack, and as long as the vacant space. In the top of this 'table' I cut six holes of 2 in. diameter, in two rows of three, and the bottoms of the cups drop neatly into these. I covered the floor level of the whole rack with white Formica; and with the cup 'table', and all the plates lifted out, it only takes a second to wipe clean.

Adjustable
Stove

While on the subject of the galley, there is another job to be done, should a non-gimballed stove be fitted. On my boat, the two-burner-and-grill Calor gas fitment is recessed into a box, so that a Formica-topped lid goes on top when the stove is not in use. On the inside top of the two athwartship sides of the box I screwed a strip of heavy gauge alloy the whole width of the box. The alloy was first bent, in profile, to roughly the shape of a question mark, the curved part bowing out away from the side. The top of the curve was drilled with $\frac{1}{4}$ in. holes at 1 in. spaces. The lower, straight part of the question mark was screwed to the side of the box.

I bought some $\frac{3}{16}$ in. brass rod, cut it into lengths just short of the distance across the box, and heated and hammered the ends gently to make a slight turn down. The two rods, bridging from side to side across the top of the stove, in a fore and aft direction, can be dropped into place on each side of any pot or kettle, and hold it firmly in position. There are sufficient holes to accommodate any size of pan (Fig. 22).

A Book Shelf

One thing sadly lacking on my yacht was a book shelf. As I ventured farther afield I collected more 'Pilots'; and although it had been possible in the beginning to tuck essentials such as Reed's under a bunk cushion when not in use, once the number of books needed on board had passed the half a dozen mark, this became impracticable. Unfortunately, it was very difficult, when the necessity arose, to even imagine where to put such books.

The only possibility seemed to be one of the 'pockets' over the quarter berths. There were two over each of these; and I call them pockets for want of a better word, and because they are similar in shape and use to the 'pockets' which motor car manufacturers fondly imagine as being useful to the motorist when placed in the dashboard. They are shaped like elongated basins placed on their sides, moulded in over the bunks, just under the side decks. In front of each pair is a plywood panel pierced with elliptical holes, smaller than the circumference of the pocket which it covers, this making a fiddle to prevent things falling out. (Fig. 23)

A better term than pocket is possibly 'glory hole', for like those in cars, they are fairly useless except for the odds and ends which may one day come in useful. There were, of course, immediately disadvantages apparent in trying to turn one of these spaces into a bookshelf. The first was that the oval cut-out in the plywood fascia was not high enough to take average books upright. Another was that, although the G.R.P. basin itself was high enough to take all but outsize books, it was not deep enough. So that it was not possible to insert the books through the fascia diagonally then stand them upright. Yet another snag was that basins do not have parallel sides. The pockets were wider at the mouth than at the back, so that there was no level platform for books to stand on. In fact, this disadvantage turned out, when I started, to be a positive advantage, after all.

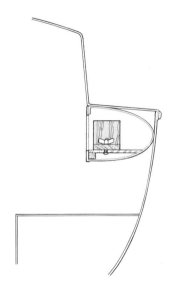

Fig. 23   Section in way of moulded locker

I made, in fact, a platform for the books from a piece of mahogany faced marine plywood. This was trimmed, its outboard corners rounded and the short sides cut in as necessary, to take up the shape of the G.R.P. basin at the lowest possible horizontal level from the back, or outboard, of the basin. With this platform in position, the front, or inboard edge was nearly an inch above the lip of the basin. The platform, with a straight front edge, extended 2 in. into the cabin, which I calculated was enough for it to take the Channel Pilot. It was propped up by an inch-thick strip of wood, the length of the straight part of the bottom lip of the basin; it was unnecessary to make it longer and shape the ends into the curve, for in fact the inward curve of the basin itself held the platform in position. The 1 in. thick × $\frac{3}{4}$ in. strip was screwed and glued under the plywood platform, set back from the edge so that it rested on the G.R.P. Now I cut two pieces of $\frac{1}{2}$ in. mahogany—one of them 4 in. square, the other 4 in. × $1\frac{1}{2}$ in. The smaller was glued to the larger to make an 'L'-shape— when working with small offcuts of hardwood, don't forget how essential it is to use the correct size drills for guide holes. The top of

the 'L' was rounded off, and eventually a piece of thin plastic foam
was glued to the large outside face. This was the same foam as used
to line the binocular box in Chapter 8.

In the centre of the short leg of the 'L'—the base—I drilled a $\frac{5}{16}$ in.
hole and obtained to fit it a $\frac{1}{4}$ in. chromium bolt with a round head
and wing nut, 1 in. long (Fig. 24). This was not a coachbolt, and
stainless steel, brass or bronze would do equally well. The next step
was to drill a $\frac{3}{8}$ in. hole in the platform. With the platform in position
in the pocket, I marked the position of this hole at the aft end, 3 in.
from the front edge and 1 in. from the end. Then, with a scribe, I
traced two lines from the hole, parallel with the front or inboard edge.
They subtended from the outside diameter of the hole, and were
therefore $\frac{3}{8}$ in. apart. The double line was taken to within 4 in. of the
other end of the platform, and the wood between cut out to make a
long slot.

The slot can be cut with a keyhole saw between two holes, one at
each end, or by drilling a whole series of holes, as close together as
possible, and joining them up with a saw or chisel. The second
method, though quicker, makes a rougher job, and a fair amount of
work with a thin flat file is necessary to make the edges of the slot
smooth. The bolt is passed up through this slot, the head downwards,
and through the hole in the base of the mahogany 'L'. The wing nut
tightens the two together when necessary, but when it is loose the 'L'
can slide up and down the slot. Because the front lip of the platform
is raised above the surface of the G.R.P. basin, the bolt head is not
causing any friction with the fibre glass. In my case, the platform was
raised an inch above the basin lip. It may not be so in every case
even where a similar arrangement is used by the builders. Check
again the thickness of the front strip of wood, then take the whole
platform and its appurtenances out, and replace the original plywood

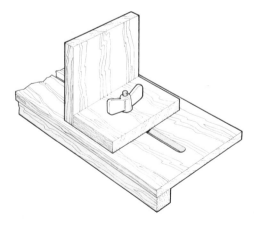

Fig. 24   Part of bookshelf

front, putting in one or two of the screws, but tightly.

Using a sharp instrument, such as the point of a sheath knife blade, scratch a line on the *inside* of the fascia, all round the inside edge of the basin. A certain amount of contortion may be needed for this. Take off the fascia again, then measure up 1 in., or whatever the thickness of the levelling up strip, from the bottom mark, and draw a

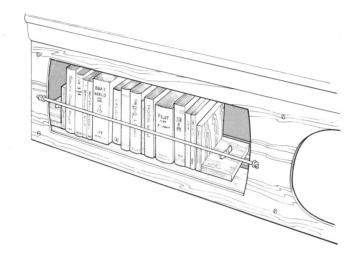

Fig. 25 Complete bookshelf with holder of shock cord

straight line on this level. Scribe straight lines all round, using on the other three sides the ends of the arcs as the ends of the lines. When the wood is cut away along these lines, the plywood front will cover the top and sides of the basin, and along the bottom it will cover the strip of wood which supports the platform, while the front edge of the platform juts out beyond it. The fascia, in fact, is all which is needed to keep the book platform in position and to stop it coming out of the hole when a book is removed, or when the boat heels.

A similar adjustable 'L' can be made for the other end of the bookshelf, if preferred. I did not do this as the other end of the pocket I used was already squared off by the side of a hanging locker, the construction of which is described in the following chapter. A length of shockcord with metal hooks was used to keep the books in position (Fig. 25). One end hooked in permanently, but the hook at the other end opened out to a right angle, so that it can easily be pulled out and pushed into a small hole drilled in the fascia. I had considered a more elaborate system with a drop bar in front of the books, but felt that this was more likely to be broken in a confined space and a heeling cabin.

10 Replacing a useless locker with a hanging locker, while increasing apparent space. Using odd corners to make a cutlery drawer. A covered tray for navigational instruments.

I consider that far and away the most important job done on my own glass fibre sloop was the construction of a hanging locker. This is a facility which most small boats lack—though one or two builders have, in some miraculous fashion, managed to produce 21 ft. yachts with both a hanging locker and a separate toilet compartment —and four berths!

In the yacht not built with these amenities it is far easier to do something about privacy for the toilet—important even in these days when mixed crews are on board—than about a hanging locker. But without the latter there is literally nothing to do with wet oilskins when leaving the cockpit, other than throw them overboard. In fact, after one more than usually normal summer, during which I seemed constantly to be struggling out of wet gear in the cockpit, stuffing it into an outside locker, and then diving below with jersey already soaked from rain and spray, I decided that something simply had to be done.

Now that I have a hanging locker in which they can dry, my oilskins seldom seem to get wet; or at least are not wet when I want to go below. But the locker comes in handy for storing shore-going rig, and does it more good than it gets from the bottom of a kitbag. My vessel is a small one, with four berths in one open cabin, and at first sight there seemed not much that *could* be done, short of discarding one of the bunks completely. The bunks, together with other moulded-in fittings, are part of the strength structure of a G.R.P. hull, and cannot be removed with impunity. If such a structure is to be removed, reinforcement of equal strength must be substituted, but I have no intention of passing out advice on this. Every type of hull is different, and a competent naval architect or surveyor should be brought in to advise in each individual case, where that sort of alteration is contemplated.

It would have been possible to build my locker on top of one of the forward bunks, and utilize the remainder of the space forward of it for storage. However, there are often as many as four people sleeping on board, and it seemed a pity to discard one berth. A further examination showed that there was an alternative. On the starboard side, amidships, there was already a locker as part of the equipment of the ship. It fitted between the end of the quarter berth, and that of the forward bunk. The space was narrow—only just over a foot—and the locker was about three feet high with a fiddle around its top surface.

This locker had proved to be a useless piece of equipment. The top was too narrow to use as a working surface, and too high to be used as a table between the two bunks. The fixed fiddle made it impossible to stand a tray on it. Below, it was divided into two compartments, one above the other, the lower with a door and the other open. It had the same depth as the bunks, so its total cubic capacity was quite large; but only items such as cutlery in a tray, tablecloths, could be stuffed into it. These left a lot of waste space, and I had been intending to fit it out with racks and shelves, or perhaps turn it into a cocktail cabinet. No small yacht can afford to have so much space not utilized to the full. It occurred to me to remove this locker altogether and replace it with the hanging locker I required. Several disadvantages were seen. One was the narrow width available between the two bunk ends. Another was that a full-height cupboard, from cabin sole to deckhead (which it had to be, to be of use with headroom of only just over five feet) right amidships might appear to fill up the cabin space. Again, one of the cabin windows extended partly across the space which would be enclosed by such a locker.

After sitting and looking at the problem for some time, I decided that it might be possible to make the locker wider than the one foot space between the bunks. And that, if so, perhaps it would not be necessary to bring it out to the gangway line. The extra width would make it easier to hang things in it, and the lesser depth would overcome, I hoped, any tendency for the height to crowd out the living space. As for the window, a wider locker would extend even farther over it, but I decided to ignore this. And in the event it has made no difference, except to let some light into the locker. Fortunately, the quarter berth on the starboard side was rather longer than six feet, and as it is my bunk, and I am only five-eight, it would be no discomfort to rob it of a few inches. The forward berth on that side is only ever occupied by a child, and was a good six feet long, so the same argument applied. I found that the small locker was held in place between the bunk ends by four nuts and bolts, two in each side. Once these were unscrewed, it lifted out easily. I was pleased to find that it was strongly made of $\frac{3}{8}$ in. marine ply, and a good deal of this wood went into the new locker.

I now noticed, for the first time, that the two bunks were on different levels, the forward one being about 3 in. higher than the quarter berth. As I meant to spread my locker over both bunks by five inches on each side, I should have to make the sides of different lengths. And because the new locker would not go down into the space between the bunk ends, as did the old one, I should have to think of a different method to anchor it into position. In fact, whereas the locker removed had been necessarily a piece of furniture in its own right, the new one had to be built in to become part of the yacht's structure. For, following the curves of hull and deckhead—which were extremely complicated—it could have no top, back or bottom— and, as a hanging space, could have no internal shelves to give it support.

Shaping the Back

The biggest difficulty was to find a method to shape the back edges of the locker's sides, where they rested against the hull, cabin top and coachroof. The small locker had abutted only against the lower part of the hull, but even so its curves were quite complicated, with both sides different. I also had to take into account the added

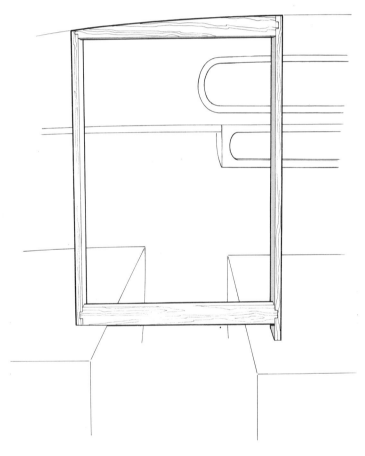

Fig. 26   Front frame for hanging locker

convolutions of the upper works; the side deck, the window, even a moulded-in wiring channel in the deckhead lining which just started to widen into a base for a cabin light at the point where one side would cross it.

I found that a Mimic Shape Tracer was very useful in getting the exact outline of the moulding around the window frame and the wiring channel, etc. The Mimic consists of hundreds of fine steel needles set side by side between two bars, with the needles, in their plane, protruding from both sides. One edge is placed against the moulding with some pressure, and the needles slide through the bars, taking up the shape. This can then be traced off on the work.

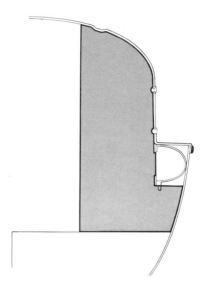

Fig. 27

However, the Mimic is only 6 in. long, so it was not much help in giving me the overall set of curves for my 4 ft. sides.

The method I eventually hit upon is rather complicated to describe, but very effective in use. I made the front frame for the locker, cutting the two uprights accurately to length and shaping the top to the fore and aft curve of the deckhead (Fig. 26). I used 2 × 1 in. hardwood for the sides, with the narrow edge facing out, and 3 × 1 in. for top and bottom rails, with the wide edge facing out. The top had to be slightly shaped, and the lower rail was at an angle of 90° from the bottom of the shortest side. As all the pieces were eventually

to be fastened securely to the bunks, hull and deckhead, I made only
shallow mortise and tenon joints. I screwed the four pieces together,
but did not glue them at this point, as I should presently have to
dismantle them again. I made this front frame accurately enough so
that it just jammed into position between the bunk tops and the
deckhead. (It is easy to get measurements accurate enough for this by
using the two-batten method, already described, and by always
cutting just outside the marks). Had the fit been sloppy, I should
have used wedges to hold it, for it is important, for the next stage,
that it will stay in position without glueing, set absolutely vertical by
means of a square.

It is worth mentioning here that all horizontals in the cabin *should*
be parallel with the waterline, but in mass production they may not
always be so. If the boat is in a cradle, or on chocks, get the water-

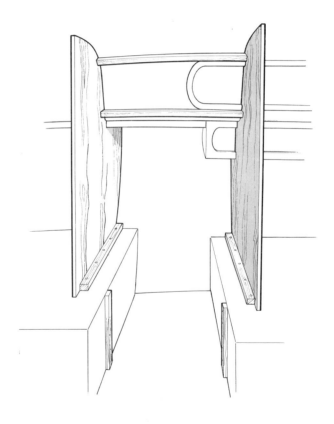

Fig. 28   Sides of hanging locker : here the lower edges were of
different height

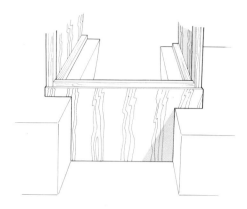

Fig. 29   Plywood dropped to cabin sole below hanging locker

Fig. 30

line trimmed horizontal, by means of a spirit level and then check
'level' surfaces in the cabin to see if they conform. Otherwise the use
of a square on the sort of job at present being described could be
meaningless.

Before the frame was put into place, the outer edge of each side
was marked off in half inches. Then, when the frame was vertical and
secure, a square and a yardstick were used to measure the horizontal
distance, at each half-inch station, between the front of the frame
and the side of the hull. These measurements were transferred to a
sheet of thick brown paper, one edge of which was also marked out
in half inch spaces. The dots thus plotted were joined up with a
pencil and the shape cut out. This in turn was traced on to a piece of
hardboard, cut out again, and then offered up. It was a reasonable fit,
but not as accurate as I wanted, so alterations were made until it was
as perfect as could reasonably be expected. It is important to do it in
these stages, as marine plywood is very expensive. If the hardboard
pattern is made for the largest side first—in this case the after side—
the same piece can then be used as a pattern, suitably trimmed down,
for the other side. (Fig. 27)

Having got the sides to the correct shape, the rest of the job was
fairly straightforward. The only other real complication was the fact
that the after side of the locker abutted against a small 'pocket'-type
locker (see previous chapter) situated just above the quarter berth. I
removed the plywood fascia to this locker, and cut it off short so
that it fitted flush with the side of the hanging locker. The G.R.P.
basin behind the fascia had, along its bottom edge, a vertical lip
about 1 in. wide and about $\frac{1}{8}$ in. thick. When cutting out the side of
the hanging locker I ignored this lip, as though it did not exist. Then,
when I was fitting the side, I cut a slot through the G.R.P. lip and
pushed the side panel into it. This helped to give valuable support
and strength, while at the same time eliminating a lot of the
difficulty of the pattern making. (Fig. 28)

It is unlikely that this exact situation will arise in other classes of
yacht; but wherever this kind of G.R.P. lip can be used for
strengthening, it should be. Care must be taken, of course, that it is
not cut into too deeply, so as to impare the strength of the G.R.P.
structure; but the wood panel or fitting can, in fact, add more than
the subtraction made by cutting. The side panels were framed in situ,
the lower pieces of $1\frac{1}{2} \times 1$ in. bolted through the bunk tops.
Another frame went in at the back of the locker, stretching between
the two sides at deckhead height, and another just below side deck
height.

The front frame, the most important, was now screwed and glued,
and a door cut to fit it. This was made of a flat sheet of $\frac{3}{8}$ in.
plywood (mahogany faced) cut slightly larger than the opening and
closing against the frame on a double ball catch. The hinges were
chrome, of the flat, outside type. The plywood door was rounded at
the corners, and strengthened by an interior frame of 1×1 in.
hardwood falling just inside the locker frame all round. Before the
door was fitted, the locker itself was fibreglass-taped to the hull,

following the procedure already described. The yacht has been subjected to strains including being lifted in and out of the water several times on slings and sailing hard to windward but there is no sign of fractures between locker and hull.

Three or four coat hooks were screwed into the upper rear frame, and some cup hooks into the lower one (which is farther back). The floor of the locker is a continuation of the cabin sole, and I drilled several $\frac{3}{4}$ in. holes in this to allow any water from wet garments to drain off into the bilge. My hope for the locker proved well founded, too. Because it does not extend out to the gangway line, but is in fact only 1 ft 10 in. deep at bunk level and much shallower at side deck level, it does not appear to intrude into the cabin in any way. On the contrary, space seems to have been gained.

Cutlery Drawer

I now, however, had to do something about the ugly space in front of the locker between the ends of the two bunks. To start with, I dropped a panel below the lower front frame to the cabin sole, (Fig. 29) bringing the plywood up to meet the bottom of the door, bolting side frames to the bunk ends and screwing the vertical panel to them. This was an improvement, but the corners of the G.R.P. bunks were rather stark. The remaining gap between the bunk ends was another waste of space, too, though on a much smaller scale than previously.

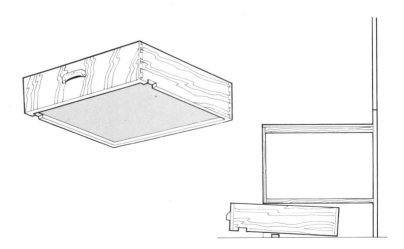

Fig. 31   Drawer under front of hanging locker

I decided to utilize it by building in a cutlery drawer, with above it a tray for my navigational instruments. The tray to be covered by a lifting top, which would make a rather narrow seat.

I made a hardwood frame of $1\frac{1}{2} \times \frac{1}{2}$ in. wood to fit the space between the bunk ends. (Fig. 30) This was merely glued and pinned together, and holes drilled through it, and through the bunk ends, the frame being fastened in place with 1 in. woodscrews driven into hardwood blocks behind the G.R.P. These blocks were set with Araldite, so that if the screws have to be removed at any time, their anchorage will remain in place.

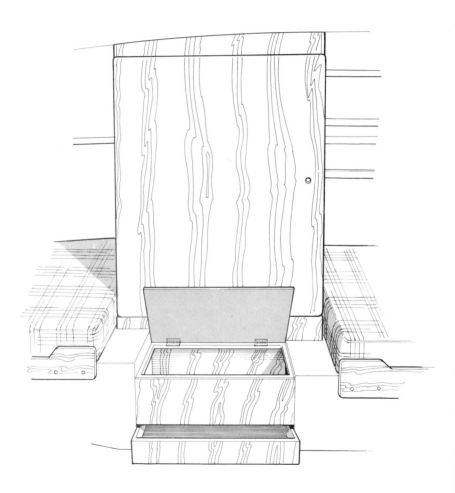

Fig. 32   Completed locker assembly on starboard side

This frame, incidentally, was made with the narrow edge of the wood upwards. I now made a similar one with the narrow edge sideways, and fixed this in position in the same manner, but about 4 in. lower. On top of this last frame was pinned a panel of $\frac{1}{8}$ in. ply, cut to shape, to make the bottom of the instrument tray.

Below this space remained a space about 6 in. high, and it was a simple matter to make a drawer of the correct width and depth to fit this exactly (Fig. 31). Front, sides and back of the drawer were of $\frac{1}{2}$ in. wood, and I cut a groove all round on the inside, $\frac{1}{4}$ in. from the bottom, in which to set a $\frac{1}{8}$ in. plywood bottom. All four sides of the

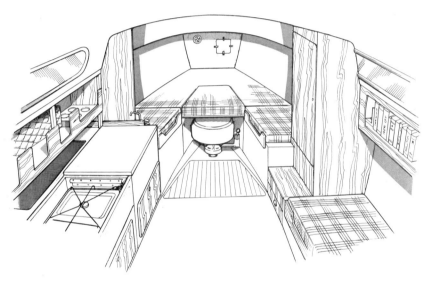

Fig. 33   Looking forward with hanging locker and drawers below it complete. Note narrow part bulkhead forward of galley for use with curtain and position of lavatory which was later concealed

drawer were made $\frac{1}{4}$ in. lower than the space they were to fit, to allow for it to be stopped. The sides were dovetailed into the front, for a drawer with a stop is bound to be pulled hard against the stop sometimes, and a simple glue line on $\frac{1}{2}$ in. timbers might well split. Having made the drawer, I cut a panel of mahogany faced plywood to cover both the drawer front and the front of the tray above it. This was cut across flush with the lower edge of the bottom frame. The top section was then glued and pinned into position and then, with the drawer pushed home, the second piece justified and fastened over it. A 1 in. hole was drilled in the centre of the drawer front as a finger pull. The next job was to cut a panel of the marine ply to fit over the top tray and hinge it to the back rail of the frame.

Putting a stop on the drawer is quite a simple business. The bottom panel was grooved in $\frac{1}{4}$ in. up from the bottom, so there was in effect a $\frac{1}{4}$ in. rail all round. On each side, 1 in. from the front, I cut a $\frac{3}{8}$ in. wide slot $\frac{1}{4}$ in. deep, then cut a length of hardwood exactly the width of the drawer and planed it to a fraction less than $\frac{1}{4}$ in. square section. Through this I drilled two countersunk holes, drilled through the G.R.P. deck below and screwed the rail down into wooden pads. This 'stop' must match up in position with that of the slots in the bottom of the drawer, when the latter is closed. Positioning the rail can be tricky, and is best done with exact measurements. The front edge of the rail should be hard against the front edges of the slots when the drawer is pushed right home. The clearance between slot and stop rail is then sufficient to allow the drawer to slide forward until the front plywood panel is clear of the matching panel above it. The drawer can then be lifted over the stop and pulled out. It may be necessary to shave the top edges of the drawer sides slightly so that they will run between the top frame and the stop. But once a good fit is obtained, the drawer cannot slide out when the boat heels.

All that remains is to sand down all the new wood and varnish it. With a 3 in. brass clock and barometer on the side of the locker facing the cockpit, this small yacht looks more ship-like than it ever did before. There also, as I said, seems to be more room below than there was before (Fig. 32).

11

Dividing into two cabins. More tips on tools. A bulkhead forward of
the galley. Hanging a curtain without sacrificing headroom, use of
Velcro.

If you are just beginning to make parts for your boat, and are not
already used to working with tools, you will run into the same sort of
basic problems as I did. At one time I found great difficulty in cutting
through a piece of wood with an ordinary hand or tenon saw. This
worried me for years. However much I tried to follow a line, so
carefully squared off, my vertical cut always wandered while I was
concentrating on the horizontal one, and vice versa. It took a friend
to tell me that I might very likely cure this tendency if I had my saw
sharpened. This was like a revelation. I had it sharpened, and set, and
much to my surprise it started doing what I wanted it to do. Obvious
to most people, perhaps, but it just had not occurred to me that a
hard metal saw cutting wood might need sharpening with frequency.
I hadn't thought about it.

In a way, the same sort of thing happened over my hanging
locker. For another awkwardness about a small yacht is the lack of
privacy for the marine toilet—an awkwardness increasing in my case
each season as my daughters grew alarmingly into womanhood, and
my sons started bringing girlfriends on board. My wife thought I
should do something about it. But what on earth *was* to be done?
The toilet sat firmly on the centre line between the two forward
bunks, nicely covered by a cushion when not in use. There was no
way of building a little room around it. Nor was there anywhere else
to shift it to. (Fig. 33)

Sitting admiring my new hanging locker, however, it one day
occurred to me that at least a partial solution was possible. The
forward side of this locker came exactly opposite the forward edge of
the galley unit. Suppose I were to put in a full height panel on the
forward side of the sink, I could hang a curtain between this panel
and the locker; a curtain which would clear the toilet by nearly a
foot. Such a panel would also divide the sink unit neatly from the
head of the forward bunk on the port side; and if it were set back
from the alleyway the same distance as the locker was set back on
the starboard side, it would lend an air of symmetry. Would it, though,
shut in the accommodation and make it seem much smaller, in a way
which the locker had failed to do?

It was worth trying, anyway. For the hanging locker, plywood panels had been quite thick enough, as the whole thing formed a box girder supporting itself. This new panel had to rely upon itself for support, however, so I needed something thicker, and decided to use $\frac{1}{2}$ in. birch veneered chipboard. As in the case of the locker sides, it would rest on the forward bunk which abutted on the galley unit; but would be relatively simple as it could be screwed directly to the galley unit, which was itself built of $\frac{1}{4}$ in. ply.

The same method as before was used for marking out the contours of the hull side. This time the task was slightly more difficult, owing to the added thickness of the panel; the inward sweep of the bows at this point was sharp enough to make a noticeable difference in sections $\frac{1}{2}$ in. apart. It meant that the inside edge of the panel had to be chamfered just at the right angle throughout to get a good fit—a matter of repeated trial and error. Once the chipboard was cut, I used it as a pattern to mark out two 'opposite twin' pieces of white Formica. This I cut with the special Formica cutting blade which fits in the handle of my Stanley padsaw. I have described the use of this tool in Chapter 4.

The only edge of the chipboard to show once the panel was in place was the vertical one on the gangway. This could have been covered with a narrow strip of Formica, glued on in the same way; but I used a capping of mahogany, which looks more seamanlike. I cut this to length and planed it, but did not screw and glue it into position until the panel was in place.

Because this panel could be screwed into the end of the galley unit, which would give it ample support, I did not think it necessary to use tape and resin to fasten it to the hull. I offered the panel up and marked the position of its edge against the hull with a pencil; roughened a strip the width of the chipboard across the deckhead down to the bunk top, and then coated the edge of the panel liberally with Araldite. The panel was pushed carefully and tightly into position, screwed home into the sink unit, and surplus glue wiped off. When this was dry I ran triangular polythene beading all round the join between panel and hull, on both sides of the panel, to hide some of the inadequacies. The beading was stuck on with Evostik; remember to give the polythene a brisk rub with white spirit before applying glue to it.

The surface of this panel on the galley side—looking from aft forward, that is—gives a bright and sparkling appearance. My 'mate' immediately screwed a kitchen towel rack, and one for the cooking implements to it. Instead of closing the accommodation in and restricting it, it seems to open it up and promise more space than there is. This, I think, is because the opening between panel and locker is quite wide, and while it allows a vista through into a 'forward cabin', it does not quite allow you to see how small this is. The subconscious is almost persuaded that there may be several staterooms up there somewhere. Of course, not every boat has its galley placed in the same position, and if, in making this division of a small yacht the panel should fall between two bunk heads, it will probably be better to use mahogany surfaced chipboard, to be varnished, rather than covering it with Formica. Though some of the simulated wood grain laminates are very suitable. For my purpose the white melamine proved ideal, for it is easily wiped down if splashed with fat whilst cooking.

Privacy

Now I had the hanging locker on one side and the galley screen on the other, both set back from the alley way line made by the bunks. However, the object of the second part of this building programme had still not been achieved; people using the toilet had no more privacy than before.

The next step, then, was to hang a curtain between the two, to complete the 'bulkhead'. (Fig. 34)

I bought a length of curtain rail from Woolworth's, with the necessary brackets, gliders, stops and so on. It had been obvious from the inception of this idea that the rail could not be screwed directly into the deckhead; the holes in the brackets are too small to take Rawlnuts; and there was, in any case, a stronger and more satisfactory way of doing the job.

This was to fix a wooden beam as a span between the locker side and the galley screen, to use as an anchorage for the curtain rail. This would take no more headroom, as the rail would be fixed not under but beside the beam; and by fixing the rail on the foreside of the beam, the latter would act as a pelmet for the runners and hooks.

I call it a 'beam', but it had to be of the smallest possible section, and I found that it need, in practice, be only 1 in. deep by $\frac{3}{4}$ in. wide. I bought a piece of knot-free obeche of this section, 8 ft long. This was cut to the width of the cabin, at deckhead level, at that point.

The deckhead, of course, is a concave curve from below; and that curve proved to be such that the wood would not bend sufficiently to fit closely along its whole length; not without risk of splitting. So I made cuts from the top edge downwards, through just over half the depth, one at every $\frac{1}{2}$ in. centre. The next step was to drill two holes at each end, through the width, to take $1\frac{1}{4}$ in. woodscrews, gauge 6, 18 in. apart. These were for screwing the 'beam' to the locker and to the galley screen—into the forward sides of both. The holes, of course, were countersunk. Next, with a flexible batten, I made a pencil mark on the deckhead to show where the beam would come, and then scraped and roughened the fibre glass. Then I cut three shores from rough timber, one to reach from deck to deckhead, dead centre, the other two to reach from the bunk tops to a point about half way between centre and inside edges of locker and galley screen. I had plenty of wedges handy from previous jobs.

For this job, I mixed up a good quantity of Araldite; it is no good skimping here, as adhesion is all important. Coating the top of the beam liberally, I held it centrally against the bulkheads and brought the centre shore into position, pushing the beam up against the deckhead. This is definitely a job for two people; one to hold the beam to see that it does not twist over on to its side as the curve is pushed into it; the other to get the shore into position, and drive in wedges. The two side supports were brought up in the same way. A great deal of care was needed, as the 'beam' very much wanted to take the line of least resistance, and twist on to its side. But the saw cuts allow the wood enough flexibility, so that it will bend the required amount without breaking.

As soon as the three supports were safely wedged in position, I drove the screws into the galley screen and locker. It is best to tighten the inner one on each side first. Wooden pads behind the locker sides enabled the screws to get a better grip than they could have done in ply alone. Once the beam was held absolutely rigid, I rubbed surplus glue into the now 'V'-shaped saw cuts along the beam.

The shores should be left in position for at least 48 hours, and it is better if they can be left for a whole week, particularly if the temperature is low. They can then be removed, and the support brackets for the curtain rail screwed into the forward side of the beam. Fixing the rail is then a simple matter of following the

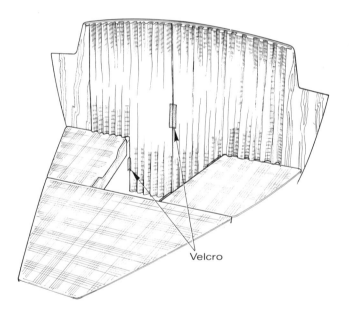

Velcro

Fig. 34

instructions—or would be in any normal 'shore' situation for which the rail is fabricated.

I used Woolworth's curtain rail, as I said. This is an 'I'-shaped girder, and it was not until I came to put it up that I discovered it was plastic-coated metal, not solid nylon. Because of its shape, while it would bend as much as desired on a horizontal plane, it would not bend at all on a vertical one. And because of the concave curve in the beam which I had just fixed, it *had* to be able to follow that shape.

The only answer was that which had served for the wooden beam—a series of saw cuts along the top edge, this time using a hacksaw. This did the job very well; the rail bent as desired, and as there was to be little weight in the curtains, it did not matter that some strength had been sacrificed.

The Curtains   When the curtains are made, they too must have their top edge curved to the shape of the deckhead. I also had mine made (by a clever daughter) with the bottom edge shaped to the bunk and floor, for I did not want huge wads of curtain filling the narrowing space by the toilet. So, when closed, they reach only down to bunk level over the bunks, and to floor level over the floor.

The only snag about this proved to be that, when the boat is heeling nicely on a beat, the narrow central strip of curtain tends to hang to one side and reveal that which it is intended to keep private. I cured this by taking two 6 in. lengths of Velcro, glueing one side of one piece to the bunk vertical and sewing the other to the curtain. In all normal conditions, this ensures that the curtain fills the space. A similar length of Velcro pins the central edges of the curtains together.

If I want to tuck the curtains right away behind the partitions, the Velcro is easily pulled free.

For those who have not yet come across this miracle substance, Velcro consists of two furry-looking tapes. In fact, the fur on one tape consists of hundreds-per-square-inch of nylon hooks, while on the other it is hundreds of nylon loops. When the two are pressed together, hooks become entangled with loops, and hold very firmly. A determined pull, however, forces the hooks to straighten momentarily, and the tapes part with a tearing sound. But no damage is done, and the device will operate indefinitely. Velcro is not quite so secure as a zip fastener; it wouldn't do, perhaps, as the only fastening of a lady's dress. But on the other hand it doesn't jam or stick; and it has many uses, holding curtains in position being just one. Most good drapers stock it.

12

Preventing condensation in the G.R.P. cabin. A simple means of making glass fibre decks safe to the tread.

However comfortable the interior of a G.R.P. yacht is made with additional fixtures and fittings, it still suffers from a serious disadvantage, which it shares with steel and aluminium. That is, condensation. Two or three people sleeping in a small G.R.P. yacht can generate what seems to be pints of water, all of which condenses on the deckhead and hull, runs down and soaks clothes, blankets and food.

On warm nights, of course, hatches can be left open; but warm nights are few and far between in European waters, and there is usually some chance of rain. Moreover, when at anchor with the tide running against the wind, any rain blows straight down into the cabin unless the washboards are up.

Because of this it is a good idea to have a boom tent, or at least a length of canvas which can be slung over the boom and lashed down to the cockpit coaming. I had a stout cockpit cover made to protect the varnish when no-one is aboard, and this doubles very well at night. Slung over the boom, it enables the washboards to be left out, no matter what the weather.

Even this does not prevent condensation, however, and the only satisfactory answer is to line the inside of the hull wherever it shows within the accommodation space. There is no point in lining the bilges, though it is a good idea to cover the back of lockers where clothes or food are kept. Don't forget that, if 99 per cent of the hull is lined, the other 1 per cent will act as an overworked condenser, and pour water out of the atmosphere like a dripping tap. One area easily forgotten is that under the quarter berths—particularly the deckhead there, which will remain cold because it is, on the other side, the deck of the cockpit lockers.

There is a traditional way of overcoming the condensation problem which has been used on steel ships for generations. This is one of the anti-condensation paints, which for the most part are ordinary paint into which quantities of cork granules have been mixed. When applied, and dry, the cork acts as an insulator. An example is 'Korkon' made by International Paints.

More modern are the 'hairy' paints, which deposit long nylon fibres over the surface. At the time of writing I have seen these advertised only in the automobile press; but no doubt they will soon appear in marine chandlery lists, and should serve well as anti-condensants. My own preference, and the method used on my own yacht, is for quilted plastic sheets—the stuff sold for bed headboards, and so on. It consists of two sheets of polythene between which is sandwiched a thin layer of plastic foam, the whole held together by the quilted pattern. This, of course, makes an excellent insulation, and cuts down condensation completely. It is available in many different colours, and is not too expensive.

Two Conditions The only disadvantage it has is the conditions necessary for it to adhere successfully to the G.R.P. They are (a) that the hull must be absolutely dry and (b) that it must be absolutely clean. Both conditions are hard to fulfil. While you are working in the cabin to fix the material, your breath is condensing on the hull, which is being cooled by water or air outside. And the interior of the hull has been coated with some sort of emulsion paint which the adhesive used for the plastic will peel off in chunks. Removing this paint from the whole of the inside surface is a good deal harder than just removing it over a few square inches where it is desired to stick a wooden block.

As far as dryness is concerned, it is essential to do this job on a really warm summer's day—*not* during the winter. Have the boat on a hard, or high and dry anyway, so that cooling water is not making the hull into a condenser, and let the sun thoroughly warm up the interior. The paint is most easily removed with a wire brush; and it will make the job even more simple if an electric drill with a rotary wire brush attachment is available.

The plastic quilted material is sold in most do-it-yourself shops and ironmongers in 2 ft widths, so it is necessary to work out what area will be wanted, and then convert this to the necessary number of yards or metres length. The lining is also sold with or without a self-adhesive backing. I have used both, and have never, personally, been able to persuade the self-adhesive stuff to adhere satisfactorily for long. It always, in my experience, goes dog-eared at the corners. It is fair to say, however, that other people tell me that they use it and have no trouble. Using that with the plain, non-stick back, I use Cow gum to stick it to the hull. This is a plain rubber solution, and if applied to both surfaces and allowed to dry slightly, it grips well though it is not an impact glue. This means that the material can be moved about until it is aligned properly. It can also be peeled off at some later date, if necessary, without leaving a lot of the plastic adhering to the G.R.P. This could be useful if the hull ever needs repair. The pieces should be cut to shape and fitted before sticking down, and it is worth leaving an overlap of about $\frac{1}{16}$ in. as the plastic material shrinks about this much very quickly. Punch holes to allow chainplate bolts to come through, and also where other fittings are bolted through the deck. Do not try to mould the material around these protuberances; this only makes pockets of air which become moisturized, and soon starts the material peeling away in sheets.

Deck Paint   While discussing paints for special purposes, the problem of glass fibre decks is worth underlining. G.R.P. with a normal gel coat literally is as smooth as glass, and nothing could be more dangerous on the deck of any yacht. Some more expensive yachts overcome the problem by laying strip planking on top of the G.R.P. deck. This is out of the question for most of the craft we are dealing with here, and the moulders often try to make the deck 'non-slip' by incorporating a piece of Trakmark or a similar pattern into the mould, to give a 'rough' finish.

The result is only better in small degree than if the moulding had been left smooth, and going forward when water is on the deck remains a hazardous operation; the smaller the boat, the more hazardous. It is therefore essential to have a truly non-slip surface anywhere that people might stand including the coachroof and this a G.R.P. moulding can never give. Grit or pumice should have been introduced into the gel coat when the yacht is built, but the best answer if this has not been done for an owner is to paint. A new type of paint has recently come on to the market to deal with this. The one which I have tried myself is 'Helmsman' Non-slip Deck Paint, a thixotropic polyurethane based product, containing ground-up pumice stone. Because it is a 'jelly' paint, the pumice does not sink in the tin, and no stirring is necessary.

The surface, when dry, provides a first class gripping surface which, surprisingly enough, is quite comfortable to bare feet. It can be kept clean by scrubbing, without difficulty. Application of this paint follows the rules laid down in Chapter 7. The surface must be thoroughly degreased and cleaned, and then etched with an etching primer. Then the paint is applied as thickly as possible, no attempt being made to obliterate brush marks.

During the season the paint surface will chalk slightly, and cleaning will thin it out, so that new paint can be applied the following year, without too much of a build-up. This paint can be used in the cockpit, too, where a slippery deck is an equal danger. But there is a much better solution here, and this is described in a later chapter.

13 Replacing the standard G.R.P. sliding main hatch cover with one built of hardwood. The simple way to obtain a professional looking job. A simple steam chest.

One of the criticisms most often made against G.R.P. yachts is that they look like bathtubs—never mind what they sail like. It is, of course, only the small craft which come in for this stricture; the large custom-built jobs, and even the expensive standard production yachts over say 35 ft., can have teak decks laid over the glass fibre, and with teak capped rails, coach roof trimmings, and so on, there is not really much difference in appearance between a G.R.P. and a traditional yacht. But it is the smaller G.R.P. yachts we are concerned with here, where there is not much opportunity for the use of wood, even if the builders thought the added expense justified. For, don't forget, the great thing about the small production G.R.P. craft is that it would cost twice as much were it built of timber in the traditional way.

A whole mass of glass fibre, more or less unrelieved, does present a rather cold, unshiplike appearance—in the eyes of the traditionalist, at least, Of course it does not really matter. What counts is whether the yacht sails well enough for its owner, whether it is seaworthy, comfortable and safe. But unfortunately, being human, we also have false pride, and the important things are not always enough. We want our yacht to have a more pleasing appearance. There are various ways of achieving this, and it is surprising what a difference can be made by discarding the G.R.P. sliding hatch over the main companionway, and making a wooden one to replace it. Such a simple device alters the whole appearance of the yacht, so that if it were not for the sail insignia, it would be practically unrecognizable. A few builders in the past realized that a wooden hatchcover makes all the difference. But I notice that most of these have gone back to G.R.P. recently, undoubtedly on the grounds of expense. Small yachts have become so much dearer to build in the past few years, that the yards dare not add unjustifiable costs.

One Proviso   However, for the handyman with tools, there is no real difficulty in making a hatch cover. The only proviso is that it must be made well. I have seen one or two home-made jobs which would have been better not made at all—they detract from rather than enhance the appearance of the boat. The wood to use for this, of course, depends on what finish any other exterior woodwork has—grab rails on the coachroof, washboard and locker seats. It will be either teak or mahogany, and on the whole mahogany is easier to work and gives a rich glowing appearance when finished. Teak, on the other hand, is more shiplike; but it is very expensive. Afrormosia, or African teak, can be used instead; there is not much difference in appearance, but it is rather harder to work than Burma teak, the grain running every which way in places.

Every yacht builder seems to have a different method of fastening down his sliding hatch covers, and of course it is usually best to apply to the wooden hatch the method used for the G.R.P. one. It is, however, possible that when the method by which the G.R.P. hatch adheres to its slides is examined, it will be found better to alter it completely. This will mean extra work on the coachroof, but may be essential.

Fastening Down

I can only describe here the method by which my own hatch was secured to its slides. I found it unsatisfactory for the wooden one, but only a slight modification was needed. The difference arose in my case because of the difference in thickness of materials. Whereas the G.R.P. hatch was a more or less uniform $\frac{3}{16}$ in. throughout, the wooden one had obviously to be much more substantial, the skirt being $\frac{7}{8}$ in. thick. The way the G.R.P. hatch was held down was as follows. On each side of the opening a substantial G.R.P. box beam supported a brass strip, screwed into it, which overhung the outboard side of the beam by $\frac{1}{2}$ in. The hatch cover itself was a G.R.P. lid with skirts all round. Out of the skirt at each end was cut two squares to fit over the beams, an outboard slot at the top of each square to take the brass strips. The sliding cover was held, therefore, only at each end. (Fig. 35) There was naturally a gap between the side skirts of the cover and the beams, and had a 'green one' ever broken over the coachroof, a great deal of water would inevitably have found its way up and over the beam and into the cabin.

I had never noticed that this was the way it was done until I began to make the wooden cover. I then decided that the new one must be held in place along its whole length, not just at each end. This would not only be safer—I knew all about the suction power of a big wave breaking over the boat, and imagined how it would pluck off and throw away a cover held only at four points—but it would stop a good deal of the water which would otherwise find its way in from a lesser wave breaking over the cabin. A difficulty immediately made itself apparent, however—a difficulty which may not arise on a boat of any other marque. But it provides an example of the sort of thing one always comes up against, and how such difficulties are only made to be overcome.

I found, in fact, that there were two brass strips, not one, on each side of the opening. For the beams carrying the runners were bisected by another beam running athwartships just on the fore side of the opening. This was obviously an important strength member for the coachroof; it was thicker and deeper than the two fore and aft beams. On each side there was therefore one brass strip aft of it and one forward of it. The transverse beam stopped the hatch sliding too far forward or aft.

The important thing about this beam was that while the G.R.P. skirts of the original cover cleared it, the thicker ones of my wooden hatch would not. This could be overcome by making the hatch slightly wider; but in that case I still could not have the side skirts gripping along their whole length.

The only way to get over it was to cut away the ends of the transverse beam so that the two longitudinal beams were clear along their whole length. I gave the matter due consideration and decided that it would not effect the structural strength enough to worry about, and that some added strength could in fact be added to replace that lost.

The ends of the beam were therefore cut away with a metal-cutting keyhole saw. This revealed that the beam was in fact hollow, and that it extended underneath the coachroof, outboard of the hatchway. (Fig. 36) Into the space I therefore pushed some lengths of $\frac{1}{2} \times \frac{1}{2}$ in. hardwood, drawing them back until they bridged across the area which had been cut away. I then mixed some resin and hardener and poured it in on top of the wood—not enough to fill all the hollow space, but enough to cement and bind the wood to the beam. This was done on both sides, of course. (Fig. 37)

The hole on top and side of the beams was then filled in with polyester paste, and when this had set, sanded down to make a

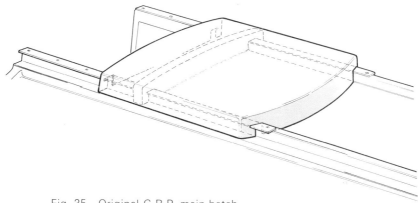

Fig. 35   Original G.R.P. main hatch

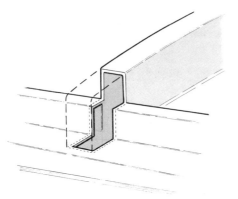

Fig. 36   Hollow beam under hatch showing part cut away

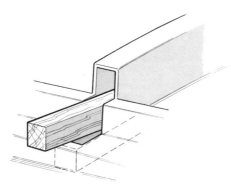

Fig. 37   Hardwood stiffener inserted

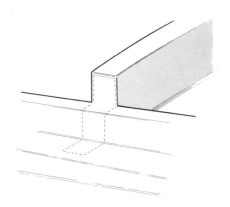

Fig. 38   Opening glassed over and sealed flush

smooth continuous surface with the rest of the longitudinal beams.
(Fig. 38) The next step was to buy continuous lengths of the brass
strip to take the place of the four short lengths, to drill and
countersink them, taking care that the holes fell in the same places
as the previous ones. This strip was then bedded down on a mastic
compound and screwed into place. It was now possible to put the
original G.R.P. hatch back in its place if necessary; and this was in
fact done while the new wooden one was being made.

Plan of Hatch   The plan of the G.R.P. hatch was roughly square, but with the
forward edge bowed. There was no real reason for the new hatch to
be other than square, but I considered the bowed front gave a better
appearance; and as I had never tried to steam timber before this

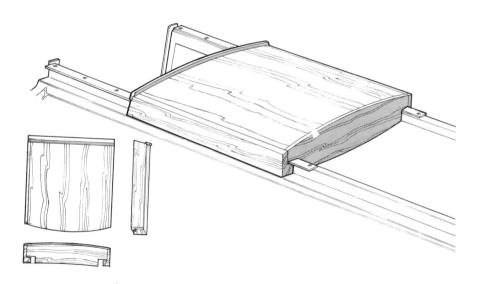

Fig. 39   The new wooden main hatch

seemed to be a good opportunity. I had obtained some 6 in. wide
planks of mahogany, unprepared 1 in. thick. So the first job was to
plane these smooth, which brought the thickness down to the $\frac{7}{8}$ in.
on which I had calculated. When taking measurements, several
things had to be taken into consideration. One was the transverse
beam which had already been a problem. The top of the hatch had to
clear this, but the closer to it the better—again to keep out any water
washing over the coachroof. Then, the coachroof itself was, of

course, cambered; the fore skirt of the cover had to take account of that, and the top of the cover itself had to be curved athwartships, to allow water to run off.

The fore end of the hatch cover therefore had to look like Fig. 39, in elevation, and plan. As the frame was to be covered with mahogany-faced marine plywood, the top edge of the frame had to be rebated all round, too.

I examined the G.R.P. hatch whilst it was in position, and noted how closely it fitted down on the transverse beam, and how near its skirts came to the coachroof top. I then removed it again and used the inside dimensions, making due allowance where I thought tolerances could be closer. On these measurements I marked out the shape of the forward skirt, making it rather longer than required to allow for the bow I hoped to put into it. The amount by which the top of the G.R.P. hatch cover curved was adequate, so I used that to mark out a brown paper pattern for the ends, and transferred it to my still flat piece of mahogany. This curve I then cut out as a series of straight cuts with a hand power saw, finishing off with a Surform tool and then a spokeshave.

The next step was to cut a rebate to take the plywood in the top edge. I thought this could have been done with a metal rebate plane, in spite of the curve. But the simplest way proved to be again with the power saw, the blade set to cut $\frac{3}{8}$ in. deep (the thickness of the plywood) and the fence $\frac{1}{2}$ in. from the inside edge. I then used the scriber to mark the $\frac{3}{8}$ in. limit down from the curved edge, put the rebate plane's fence to $\frac{3}{8}$ in., and made the cut along the inside surface. It came off as easily as you like. Rebates in the other three sides were made in the same manner (Fig. 40). Anyone who has no power saw and no rebate plane, and feels that he could not use them if he had, will be wise to forget the rebate altogether.

An Alternative Leave the top of the curve, and subsequently of the other sides, flat, and bring the plywood right out to a $\frac{1}{4}$ in. overhang all round. With the edges of the ply rounded off with sandpaper, this will look quite good, and is a method in fact followed by some shipwrights for the sake of cheapness. It doesn't take so long, and time is of course money.

I had my rebate, however, and now wanted to put a bow in the forward end. Which meant that I needed a steam chest. I made one quite satisfactorily after giving the matter a bit of thought. I had none of those pieces of 6 in. diameter pipe lying about which most writers believe that everyone finds to hand. What I did have were three 5-pint size beer cans, so using a tin opener of the type which makes a clean cut around the inside of the lip, I removed five ends, leaving only one can with one end. I drilled two small holes opposite each other in the sides $\frac{1}{2}$ in. from the lip of each can— except that which still had an end and joined them.

Tin tacks can be hammered through the holes and bent over. This will prevent the tins coming apart. The seams between each tin are then filled up with soft putty and bound round on top of it with insulation or Sellotape. For longer pieces of wood, more cans can be used. Now I needed some sort of heating device, and in fact had an old and long disused paraffin stove which my wife had been urging me to throw away for years. Which shows that everything comes in useful eventually. I then bought a cheap tin kettle from Woolworths, as electric kettles are soon ruined if kept boiling for long periods. The stove was set up and my pipe of tins suspended from the roof of the shed at an angle of about 45°, with the closed end at the top, and the bottom end near to the spout of the kettle. I cut a foot length off the plastic garden hose (the heat was too much for this, eventually, and I had to replace it with a piece of rubber hose from the household washing machine. I suffered for this later). The kettle was filled, the stove lighted, the tube led from kettle spout to inside of pipe, the wood to be bent pushed up into pipe, and the bottom end closed with rags. Making sure, of course, that the rags did not impede the exit of the steam from the hose into the tin pipe.

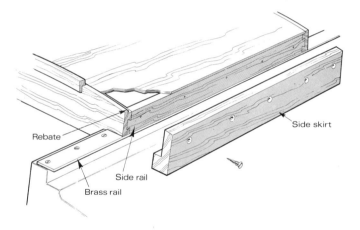

Fig. 40   Wooden hatch components

The operation took several hours, the kettle having to be refilled a number of times. Occasionally the wood was taken out to see whether it was getting any more pliable. After about four hours' steaming it was judged 'done'. Some thought had already been given as to a former, or pattern, and it was decided to use the G.R.P. cover to get the same curve. Accordingly the steamed wood was clamped on to this, using wooden pads to prevent the mahogany being marked by the clamps. The wood took up the curve relatively easily, without splitting or cracking.

This was left in the clamps for 48 hours, in a warm dry place. When the clamps were eventually removed the wood did not, unfortunately, remain in exactly the curve to which it had been set, but sprang back into a slightly shallower curve. However, this did not really matter—the front could have been left straight if necessary. I made up the rest of the frame now, taking into account dimensions from the curve we had, this being less than the G.R.P. cover, and less than the curve of the transverse beam. This meant that the side skirts of the new cover had to be longer than those of the old.

The Aft End   Anyone making a similar hatch cover for a different yacht would not necessarily have this transverse beam problem to overcome, but others of a similar nature. The rather full description being given is as an example of how such difficulties can be tackled.

The aft end of the hatch cover now had to be made, and this presented its own problems. A sideways elevation of the deckhouse showed that this had a backward slant, down to the cockpit deck, and that the aft end of the G.R.P. hatch cover followed this slant. The aft skirt, too, was deeper than the other three, meeting the top of the washboards. (Fig. 41)

These boards slid in grooves enclosed by wooden runners, the top ends of which fitted snug against the aft skirt of the cover when it was closed.

If I were to make the aft skirt of my sliding hatch vertical, there would be a gap between the bottom of the skirt and the top of the washboard through which rain would certainly run. This could be solved by cutting away the top of the washboard runners, or by making the washboards deeper, so that they came higher, at the same time making the aft skirt shallower.

However, I decided to do it the hard way, and have the aft skirt slanting at the same angle as the washboards. This meant that the overall depth from bottom of skirt to top of hatch cover had to be taken diagonally, and the edges levelled off when the framework was complete. This was simple enough. But it should be pointed out at this stage that the width of the front and back skirts was not the same as the width of the same members on the G.R.P. cover, which had been wider than necessary in order that the slits to take the brass runners should not be too near the side skirts. In this case I wanted the side skirts to be as near the rails as possible without jamming.

I therefore made front and back skirts the exact width between the outside edges of the runners, plus $\frac{1}{4}$ in. (to give $\frac{1}{8}$ in. clearance on each side). Now the side rails were made, the correct slope being cut in their after ends. These rails were the exact depth required from the top of the end pieces, to the brass rail on which they were to stand (Fig. 40).

The side rails were made the full length of the cover less half the thickness of the cross skirts. I made a dovetail from the side rails into the end rails, through half their thickness. When jointing into the after skirt, which is on a slope, keep the tail straight, making it first, then mark out the female part at the correct angle (Fig. 41).

It is important to remember that the top edge of the side skirts has to be chamfered to follow the curve of the top, so the inner edge must be level with the top of the cross rails $\frac{1}{8}$ in. from their ends. Having got all the frame made, put it together, using wedges in the dovetails if they will not hold rigid without, then offer it up to the hatchway to see if it fits. Make any adjustments necessary, even scrapping the wood and starting again if necessary. But if reasonable care and accurate measurements have been taken, there should be little wrong with it.

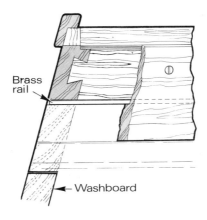

Fig. 41   Section of after end of hatch looking athwart-ships

Word of
Warning

A word of warning which I have given before. Make every measurement three times. Never take it for granted that you were accurate the first or even the second time. When you have taken it for the third time, look at each measurement again and ask yourself if that really was the one you needed to take—are you forgetting to include a surplus from which to make the dovetail, or to allow for a chamfer, or whatever?

There will be many times when that extra question will gain the answer—'No, I forgot'.

The frame sits in place nicely, everything sitting square on the brass runners, the side rails with no more than $\frac{1}{8}$ in. lap over the outside edge of the runners. The bottom edge of the fore skirt just clears the curve of the coachroof, and the aft skirt runs close to the inside of the longitudinal beams, and its bottom edge meets the top of the washboards when it is closed.

When it is sitting just right, measure the angles at the corners. It may be that the best clearance is obtained when they are not all

exactly ninety degrees. So that if you clamp them up at ninety
degrees, you will be surprised when the glue is set to find that it no
longer fits as perfectly. It doesn't matter if all the angles are not
right-angles—a few degrees out won't be noticed, for no-one is
going to take up a position exactly over the sliding hatch and
criticize an angle of 92°.

Take the frame back into the warm, mix up some glue, and glue it
together. Use corner cramps if you have them; if not, set the frame
up on a board short enough for the fore and aft skirts to overhang,
nail two pieces of 2 × 2 in. to it tight up against the side rails, then
twist some thick string around the whole thing, using a Chinese
windlass to tighten it up. Now we need the two side skirts. These
need be no more than $\frac{5}{8}$ in. thick, the full length of the cover, and an
equal depth from the top of the side rail, when it is in position, to the
coach roof, minus $\frac{1}{16}$ in. for clearance.

Mark on the inside surfaces of these a line, measuring from the
top edge the depth of the side rail, plus the thickness of the brass

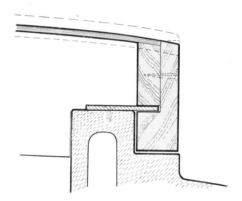

Fig. 42   Section through metal rail and side skirt of hatch

runner, plus $\frac{1}{16}$ in. clearance. Then rebate this in, above the line, the
distance by which the brass runner clears the G.R.P. beam to which
it is screwed, less $\frac{1}{16}$ in. clearance (Fig. 42 also 40). When screwed
into position, these side skirts hold the whole cover firmly to the rail.
Screw every 3 in., countersinking and covering the screw heads.
However, these side skirts cannot be screwed on finally until the
cover is put in place on its slides. The next job is to cut out the $\frac{1}{4}$ in.
marine grade plywood. Don't forget the corner angles again; if they
are not quite right-angles, cut the plywood the same. And make the
cross ship measurements *with* the curve, using a tape along the
rebate—don't measure straight across from side to side. The more

accurate this panel is cut out, the easier the next job is going to be. Use 1 in. screws, gauge 6 for this job, either bronze or stainless steel. The land is $\frac{1}{2}$ in. wide, so make a pencil scribe $\frac{1}{4}$ in. from the edge of the panel all the way round. Drill holes through the plywood at 2 in. spaces—or thereabouts, allowing for keeping the holes evenly apart, according to the length of each side. Countersink each hole $\frac{1}{8}$ in. deep.

Starting on one side, offer up the edge into the rebate, and mark the position for each screw hole on the rebate. Drill, and screw home along the whole side. Now screw home the ends in the same way, one screw at each end; bend the panel a little, the next screw at each end, and so on. It will become more difficult once the summit of the curve has been passed, and it may be necessary to use clamps— but put them on just before the screw, and then shift them up to just before the next screw, and so on. The other fore and aft edge is then fastened. Now, mark which side of the panel goes to which side of the frame, and unscrew it all again in the same order. Then replace, but this time with glue and screws. Use wood covers for the screw heads, using scrap pieces of the same plank. Leave for a week for it to set.

Planing and Sanding

Finally, any last minute planing and sanding to get a good finish can be completed. Make sure there is no spot of glue or dirt on the runners, and give them a good sanding—it is the last clean they will get for some time. Once the fit is as perfect as possible, drop the cover in position again, mix some glue, coat the side rails, and screw home the side skirts. Finally cover the screw heads.

The only other job is to fit the hasp and staple to the aft skirt (those used on the G.R.P. cover will do, but now it may be necessary to countersink inside the wooden cover for the nuts, and then give a final sanding and coat with clear varnish. It may have appeared that what we have been doing was hardly worth the effort up until this moment. But once the varnish goes on, and the grain and that rich glow start to come up—then we know that every care put into the job has been worth a fortune.

14 Overcoming the dangers of a slippery G.R.P. cockpit with a teak grating. There are substitutes, but a properly made grating will outlast the life of the ship.

Not everyone may think it worthwhile to make a wooden hatch-cover, but a number of other things may be done to improve the exterior appearance of a G.R.P. yacht; teak or mahogany capping along at least part of the cockpit coaming, for example, a teak grating for the cockpit, and so on. Yachts are as individual as their owners; and imagination is probably more important than skill with tools. A grating for the G.R.P. yacht's cockpit is an example of such an improvement. Even if a non-slip paint is used on the cockpit sole, the constant abrasion of feet often clad in sea boots, makes repainting a constant necessity. Just when a repaint is required is the time when the yacht runs into weather which results in a very wet cockpit combined with much activity in it.

I had one or two nasty experiences and was fortunate not to break a limb. I took the performance rather for granted—one of the many facets of sailing—and it was not until a friend came out for the day and pointed out what sort of dangers I was running, that I gave the matter any thought. 'Why not make a grating?' he asked. And I immediately wondered why I had not thought of it before.

There are all sorts of ways of making wooden gratings. I noticed at a recent boat show that the advertised gratings supplied with some boats—and very few bother to supply them—consist of two layers of slats cut from marine ply running at right angles to each other, and nailed together. Fine. They do the job, and are simple to make. It was something rather better and more seamanlike which I had in mind, and eventually made, however. And there is no doubt that my cockpit grating has improved the appearance of the boat out of all recognition. It is, moreover, extremely comfortable to walk on, and so non-slip that one could hardly fall off it if the boat turned turtle. Making it is simple enough, but is time-consuming and needs patience and care. I cannot help but reiterate what I have already said so many times but what is more important than ever in this case—make every measurement three times, and then stop to wonder whether you have made the right one, before actually cutting the wood. For not only is the material expensive, but to make twelve joints in one strip of wood and then find that they are wrongly spaced is the short cut to lunacy.

I made my grating from Burma teak, and sufficient to make a grating for an average 21-footer will cost about £8; but, if it is made well, the result is something which one would have to pay £30 or more for—if it were for sale. Which, as far as I know, it is not. Square or rectangular gratings are made, but not the shapes to fit cockpits of yachts—which are all odd, and all of different sizes.

I met a chap, not many months ago, who was as pleased as Punch because he had found a craftsman in a little Mediterranean port to make him a teak grating for his shower. It was five-sided, to fit the sort of corner which showers in yachts always take up; but it could not have totalled more than two square feet. My friend's pleasure was all the more acute because, as he said, he had got the job done so cheaply—it had cost him only £25!

Cockpit
Chamber
The first job is to measure the dimensions of the cockpit with accuracy. I recommend again the device of two battens, as described in an earlier chapter, as the only way to do this which will ignore the camber of the cockpit floor. The chances are that the area will have at least six angles and as many sides, so make measurements in as many directions as possible Fig. 43. There are eleven separate measurements shown.

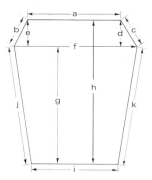

Fig. 43 Dimensions necessary to take, none of which may exactly correspond

Don't take it for granted that both sides will have equal measurements. Lay the measurements out carefully on a sheet of hardboard, then cut the hardboard out to shape, slightly proud of the lines. When this pattern is offered up to the cockpit, if it is too large it can be trimmed down, but if too small it is not so easy to rectify.

A piece of hardboard for this purpose will not cost more than 50p.—an expenditure which may save the whole cost of the wood. It checks that the measurements taken were accurate, and also makes a pattern from which to work. I used timber $\frac{3}{4}$ in. thick, which has proved quite heavy enough. I did, in fact, have difficulty in finding any Burma teak, although I was offered plenty of Afrormosia. And I was willing to buy my wood unprepared and plane it down myself. Eventually I found a timber yard with just sufficient $\frac{3}{4}$ in. teak, prepared, and so I bought that, although I had originally wanted 1 in.

The amount of timber used is exactly the area of the grating. It is a common fallacy to think that, because half the area consists of holes, only half the area of timber is needed; it is overlooked that at every cross-over two thicknesses of wood are present, which cancels out the saving in the holes. There will, of course, be a fair amount of wastage, due to all the different lengths made necessary by the odd shape. So the amount of timber actually to buy is the area h × f. Even more may have to be bought, because of the lengths of plank available; with such expensive wood, no merchant is going to sell 5 ft. out of a 6 ft. plank—the customer takes it all or nothing.

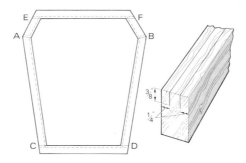

Fig. 44

Ideally, buy planks of length h and length f, in proportion to the opposite measurement. If f equals 2 ft., for instance, and h equals 3 ft., lengths of 2 ft. have to stretch down the whole of 3 ft., whereas lengths of 3 ft. have to stretch only across 2 ft. Of the 6 sq. ft. of timber needed, therefore, two-fifths of it should be in planks 3 ft. long, three-fifths in planks 2 ft. long.

The width of the planks should be somewhat proportionate to the width of the grating. For example, if f equals 2 ft., theoretically twelve 1 in. strips will be needed to fill it—they alternate with twelve 1 in. holes. But the cutting of the strips will waste at least 1 in., the width of the frame also has to be taken into account and

so does the fact that a frame is necessary. In fact, if the frame is
2 in. wide, a 14 in. plank will be necessary from which to cut two
2 in. strips for the frame, plus nine 1 in. strips for the slats, which
will have to fill 20 in. So there will be slightly more than 1 in. spaces
in this direction.

This would not be noticeable and would not matter if it were. But
in any case it is extremely unlikely that any measurement in exact
inches will ever eventuate and it will always be a case either of
spacing out, or making such exact calculations that the strips are cut
to a width which will exactly equal the spaces. I do not consider
this necessary.

Frame First   The first requirement is to take out sufficient timber for the frame.
Two inches wide is suitable for most gratings for small craft. Mark
off the short end pieces (a) and (i) on the hardboard pattern—and
measure across 2 in. from the end. The actual measurements (a) and
(i), if cut off square, would be too short—allowance must be made
for the spread, and this is where having a full-size pattern is
invaluable. Then measure off the lengths of (j) and (k), less 2 in. for
the width of (i), plus $\frac{3}{4}$ in. for two tenon joints. Similarly (b) and (c),
plus $\frac{3}{8}$ in. for one tenon joint.

Power Saw   Now, with the power saw blade set $\frac{3}{8}$ in. deep, and the fence $\frac{1}{4}$ in.
from the side, make two cuts down the inside edge of each piece of
the frame—first from one face, and then, turning it, from the other
face. Then take out a centre channel with a $\frac{1}{4}$ in. chisel, $\frac{3}{8}$ in. deep,
all round the frame. (Fig. 44)

Then make a $\frac{3}{8}$ in. mortise and tenon joint at A and B and
a tongue at C, D, E and F to fit the $\frac{1}{4}$ in. groove already made.
The correct angles can be got from the hardboard pattern. Make sure
that the frame fits together exactly to the size of the pattern. Do not
glue or fasten it at this point.

Now the remainder of the wood has to be grooved across half its
depth—scribe a line $\frac{3}{8}$ in. deep down each edge of the $\frac{3}{4}$ in. thick
planks, then mark out 1 in. grooves 1 in. apart for the whole of their
length. Cut down each line with a tenon saw, as far as the $\frac{3}{8}$ in.
scribe line, then take out the grooves with a 1 in. chisel. Teak is
quite easy to work in this way. (Fig. 45)

When all the timber is grooved, it is then cut lengthways into 1 in.
strips, and this is easiest on a saw bench or with a hand power saw.
Make sure that the saw blade is good and sharp before attempting
this job. It can be done with a hand saw of course, but give yourself
plenty of time. Any temptation to rush the job will mean badly-
fitting half joints. Turn every other strip over, and fit the half joints
together so that an oblong grating f × h is made. If the joints have
been well made, these will go together with just enough force from
finger pressure only. If some of the joints are sloppy, it doesn't
matter too much; we have resin glue to hold and fill. But if the
grooves have not been accurately spaced and cut the fractional
non-alignment of the grooves will keep doubling up and only about

half the joints will go together. Which will mean starting all over again. So—accuracy in cutting the grooves and then in the width of each strip is all-important.

Fitting the Frame   Having got the rectangular grating, place the frame on top of it. Looking through the frame, make sure that the lengthways strips are at right-angles to the ends of the frame, and that spaces, or fractions of spaces, are evenly distributed at the sides and ends. Put the hardboard pattern over the frame to check that the latter is fitted together properly, then remove the pattern and, holding the frame firmly to the grating, draw a line on the grating around the inside of the frame.

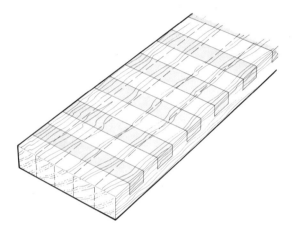

Fig. 45   First the shaded area is saw cut and chiselled out, then the piece is cut into strips as shown by pecked lines.

Remove the frame, and draw another line all round $\frac{3}{8}$ in. farther out than the first one. Cut here. We now have a grating of the exact shape but $\frac{3}{4}$ in. too big to go inside the frame. Using the first mark to cut shoulders, make $\frac{1}{4}$ in. wide tongues on the end of every strip. Because of the shape of the frame, many of the side shoulders will be cut at an obtuse angle instead of 90° (Fig. 46). Once the tongues are cut, the frame should fit on to the grating and its outside measurements conform exactly to the pattern.

I found that no pinning was necessary—glue run in the groove all around the frame held the whole thing absolutely firm. But there is no reason why every cross-over half joint, or a proportion of them, should not be glued as well if this is thought wise. The only other

filling which may be necessary is in the outside edge at the grooves
C. D. E. and F. A mixture of sawdust with glue fills such gaps
almost invisibly.

Because of the 2-in. wide frame the grating can, if slightly too
large to fit into the cockpit, be planed along its edges. If the cockpit
deck is cambered, a narrow strip of wood should be glued along the
bottom of each side, just deep enough so that both sides and centre

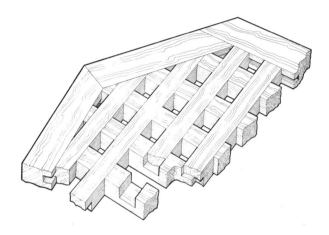

Fig. 46   Two corners of the grating

are resting firmly without rocking. The grating should not be
varnished, nor is it worth while rubbing teak oil into it, for salt water
will soon leach it out again. The natural oil in teak will preserve the
grating and ensure it a life equally as long as the yacht for which it is
made.

Teak Capping   Yet another possible improvement is the provision of a teak
capping rail to the cockpit coaming. On my craft the coaming is a
squared-off moulding about 3 in. wide. It curves inboard at its aft
end, and rises steeply to the snubbing winch platform forward. But
in between, on each side, there is a level stretch of nearly 4 ft. and it
was obviously possible to run a rail along that. I was not sure how a
part rail would look, but I thought it worth while doing it.

Luckily I had by me the split end of a consignment of teak. I had
picked it up for very little in a timber yard where it was on a
pile for burning, and had been holding it in case it would come in
handy. From it I managed to get two lengths 1½ in. thick and 3 in.
wide. I planed them, tapered and rounded off each end, and rounded
off the top corners with spokeshave and sander. Then I drilled the

rails at 1 ft centres to take $\frac{3}{8}$ in. S.S. bolts, countersinking deeply so
that the heads were well out of sight. The rails were then offered up,
the position of the holes marked on the G.R.P. coaming, and these
drilled with a $\frac{7}{16}$ in. twist drill. It was possible to reach the underside
of the coaming from the quarterberths; the space was too narrow to
get my hand in, but I used a long box spanner.

Because the inside of the moulding is domed, and very rough,
there was no point in using wooden bearing pads under the bolts, so
I used strips of alloy about $\frac{1}{8}$ in. thick which would bend as the nuts
were tightened and take up the shape. It is not generally wise to use
such dissimilar metals as stainless steel and aluminium together, but
(a) this was not important structurally and (b) it would not come
into contact with salt water to act as an electrolyte. Before putting
the bolts through, I bedded the rail down on a mastic compound,
and scraped away the squeezed out surplus as soon as the nuts had
been tightened. Mastic on the G.R.P. can be cleaned off with petrol
easily enough before it hardens.

The countersunk heads of the bolts were a good deal larger than
the screwheads for which I have already described how to punch
out wooden caps. For these bolts, then, I cut some small squares
from the teak offcuts; shaved them down with a chisel to about $\frac{1}{8}$ in.
thick, then trimmed and sanded them until they were circular and
fitted the holes. They were then bedded down on to Araldite.
Finally the rail was sanded, and given a good rub with oil. It looks
first class.

15 The many other things to remember.

Boatbuilding is no longer what it was. The small yards where a craftsman and a boy laboured for weeks—months, perhaps—to create a boat out of fine seasoned timbers, have not gone completely. But the craftsman's time, plus that of the boy, plus the cost of the timber and all the other materials which go to make up a solid timber yacht, ensure that only the few can afford to buy one.

Which in turn means that the small yard is, within comparatively few years, doomed to extinction. More boats than ever before in history are being built, because of the invention of G.R.P. But the industry is becoming even more specialized than this would seem to indicate ; what in fact is happening is that a few large firms are building G.R.P. yacht hulls, for many medium sized yards to complete. Many boatyards, in fact, no longer bother to build the hull, which is undertaken by a moulding firm. They buy the hull already moulded, complete with fuel and water tanks, very likely bulkheads, perhaps even deck and coachroof, bonded in.

Joe Bloggs buys such a hull from the Plastic Hull Division of the XYZ Co., fits it out with timber furnishings, deck fittings, masts and sails—or engine, as the case may be—and sells it as the Joe Bloggs Special. The same hull may be going to John Doe and Son's yard around the next bend of the estuary. They give it a different cabin layout, more ballast, bigger engine, and it goes into the catalogues as the John Doe Super. This comes about because of the many varied experiences and requirements of yachtsmen. Now, the XYZ Co., or its Plastic Hulls Division, quite often advertises to the private yachtsman that it is willing to sell him bare G.R.P. hulls of various sizes. Again, these can usually be bought in various stages of completion—as what is virtually a bare shell, or with bulkheads and tanks and bunks moulded in, or with all that, plus the deck moulding, and so on. The price of yachts being what it is today, it is obviously worth the while of anyone who has the time to buy the barest hull he possibly can, and finish it himself.

The bare shell will almost certainly cost a great deal less than it would cost to build a similar hull of timber in the back garden. The professionally-moulded G.R.P. job has the great advantage that its

owner knows it to be virtually impervious to water, which will not be
the case if he has built it himself.

The techniques we have discussed for fastening one thing to
another are all that need to be known in finishing off a G.R.P. hull. It
is certainly a good idea to buy the hull and the deck moulding
bonded together as one; but if a timber deck is required, the
necessary timbers can be bonded to the G.R.P. hull by the methods
described. All I can repeat here is—always degrease thoroughly;
always roughen through the resin until glass is reached over the
whole area against which the timbers will lie.

Reputation   It is as well to buy a hull from a manufacturer who has a
reputation for good moulding; there are plenty of them, all selling
something slightly different. A good check, when you see the hull
which will make the boat you want, is to ask, first:

Is the manufacturer a member of the Ship & Boat Builders
National Federation? And second: Is the hull moulded to Lloyd's
approved specifications, or under Lloyd's supervision?

The Ship & Boat Builders National Federation is the industry's
controlling body—as far as the industry can be controlled—and it
keeps a much stricter eye on standards of building and moulding
than it did at one time. So if a boat has the S.B.B.N.F. plaque or its
moulders can show in some way that the S.B.B.N.F. has given its
approval, there should not be too much to worry about.

The approval of Lloyd's Register of Shipping is even better. This
organization came to its own conclusions, some years ago, as to
just what standards of material and workmanship should go into
G.R.P. hulls. It laid those standards down quite stringently, and
any firm moulding hulls can build to them if it wishes. The specifications, or scantlings as they are properly called, are if anything
too much on the safe side.

At the firm's request, Lloyd's will send a surveyor to the yard to
check that the specifications and conditions are actually being
adhered to—and they include the humidity and temperature control
we talked about earlier, besides weight of glass, quality of resin, and
finished weights and thicknesses of different sections of the hull. If
the inspector is satisfied, he says so, and the firm may then claim
that it is building to Lloyds' approval.

Yachtsmen, generally, are rather suspicious characters, however,
and not all of them have so much trust in their fellow men that they
are willing to believe that, once the Lloyd's surveyor has gone, the
yard will not cut corners if it can. So some boatbuilders mould all
their hulls under Lloyd's supervision. This entails a Lloyd's surveyor
being at the yard all the time, or all the time during which these
Lloyd's Supervised hulls are being built. These qualified marine
surveyors, are as capable of supervising the construction of a
200,000 ton tanker as they are a 20 ft. yacht. If the yard claims that
the hull you buy was constructed under Lloyd's supervision, then
you know you are getting the best in the world. Unfortunately you
have to pay for it. The survey fees and expenses will be reflected in

the price.

The Right Hull Whatever hull you buy, make absolutely certain that it is the right hull for the job you want it to do. It is no use buying a sailing craft hull with embryo mouldings for bilge keels, if you really want a fin keel yacht; the most expert amateur cannot make that sort of alteration. Nor should you buy the hull of a motor yacht without deciding first whether you wish to have it propelled by inboard or outboard motor, or perhaps an inboard-outboard unit. (Weight distribution will be different in all cases, though it need not be too different for the second and third. But the man who wants fast speeds from an outboard, will need quite a different hull shape from that required by he who wants a good powerful inboard for amateur trawling.)

The fast outboard driven boat used for water skiing and so on is usually built with a fairly flat bottom, so that, once it gains speed, the boat rises and skims more across the top of the water than through it. And, with the weight of the engine all perched on the transom, the aft sections have to be full, in order to provide plenty of lift.

Sea Boat A good sea boat, power or sail, is usually built with a rounded bottom, and the inboard engine, main or auxiliary power, is kept away from the ends to give the hull a better balance. When completing a bare hull, the average amateur—and even many professional builders—concentrates mostly on comfortable accommodation. This is what sells boats, for it is often the part most readily appreciated by the ordinary owner. Many amateurs like to complete a bare hull not only because of the saving in cost, but because they think they can get far more comfort into a hull of given size than can the professional yacht designer.

Some years ago a yachting magazine of which I was editor held a competition in which readers were asked to plan the ideal accommodation for a hull, the lines of which were given, of about 20 ft. length overall. Somehow, within these confines, competitors managed to include spacious dining saloons besides several separate cabins; and one man even included a bathroom equipped with 6 ft. long bath, and w.c.

In fact, the accommodation will very much look after itself once the essentials are planned. If the hull is designed for an inboard motor, the bearers will no doubt already be moulded in. It is best to install the engine first, so that the business of aligning stern gear and other necessary tasks can be done with plenty of elbow room. Decide at this point about flexible mountings, universal joints and linkages, and in particular make proper arrangements for the exhaust.

Engine Size Do not install a much larger or heavier engine than the hull was designed for. It will not give more speed; in fact it may give less. At every phase of the completion it must be borne in mind that the hull was designed to a particular waterline length, at which it will give an optimum performance. If a heavier engine, tanks for fantastic quantities of fuel and fresh water, solid timber bulkheads, and so on, are installed, the hull will eventually sink well below the designed water line, and start behaving like a submarine.

Don't forget, having installed the engine, that it will not run for ever without attention; that one of these days it may even have to be lifted out for major repair. Try, then, to plan the accommodation around it in such a way that reasonable access can be gained to all parts—to the electrics and fuel leads in particular, for it is in these compartments that trouble is most likely to occur.

Ease of Maintenance   The engine is likely to have a longer life in the mechanical department if it is easy to change the oil at regular intervals, to have grease points greased, and so on. Any engine manufacturer will confirm that the working life—that is, hours run—of a marine engine is laughably short compared with that of the automotive unit from which it is probably marinized. And the difference lies in the fact that the marine version is so seldom serviced. In fact, it is often *never* serviced until it breaks down. Though a marine engine, working as it does in damp and probably salt-laden atmosphere, should be attended to much more often than a car engine. The accommodation should therefore be planned around the engine so that it can be serviced and, if necessary, removed without having to dismantle the whole of the cabin structure.

Before any of the fittings are built in, however, make provision for those things which are absolutely essential if the boat is intended to be anything but a motionless houseboat. Starting from the bows, for example, if chain is to be used for the anchor then a locker is essential, with space enough to stow at least 15 fathoms of chain. The lower this sort of weight is stowed, of course, the better, and if the hull is fairly straight stemmed, it may be possible to make a compartment in the bilge, with a hawse pipe leading up. This should have an open funnel end at the bottom. Any arrangement must be made before the forward bunks are built in, obviously.

The probability is that a modern G.R.P. hull will have a curved bow, and to get the chain into the bilge would involve having it too far aft. A compartment for it may therefore even have to be above the waterline; but do get it as far down as possible. It is also a good idea, on even a small yacht, to panel the chain locker off completely from the main accommodation. The usual type of tray in the bows of the 18 to 20 footer not only keeps the cabin smelly, but it keeps it damp, too; and some yachts even now have an old-fashioned hawsepipe, a continual ingress for wet.

Fuel tanks and fresh water tanks should as far as possible balance out the weight of the engine, so that if the latter is, as is most likely, aft of the midships line, the tanks will be forward of it—and again, of course, as low down as possible.

The best way to fabricate the tanks is to use the hull as bottom and one side, and build the other three sides of marine plywood, joining all the seams with tape and resin, and then sheathing the inside, before the top is put on, with glass mat and resin. Any tank holding more than about eight gallons, of either fuel or water, should have a baffle plate running fore and aft, and a half plate athwartships. These plates can be made of plywood, drilled with 1 in. diameter holes, and completely sheathed in G.R.P., making sure that the edges of the holes are sealed. The baffle plates are taped in, bottom and sides.

Good Pipework

Pipework must be plumbed in before the top is put on, and before the inside is sheathed. Use copper or polythene pipe, and make sure that the connections are absolutely tight ; you won't want to have to get inside the tank again to cure leaks. Bring the glass and resin well into the joints, particularly around that of the outlet pipes, leading to the pumps. The outlet will *not* be at the very bottom of the tank, of course, but lead out from the top—and don't try putting a filter inside the tank—when it blocks, as it eventually will, it will cause trouble. Have an easily accessible filter between fuel tank and pump. The fresh water supply should not need filtering.

Fuel filler inlet will either go into the tank top, but should be led down almost to the bottom. It should, naturally, go up to the deck, and as at this point the deck is probably not bonded on, and will not be until bunks and so on have been constructed over the tanks, connect flexible hose to the tank, allowing sufficient length to reach the filler nozzle in the deck when the time comes.

If the water filler inlet is in the deck, make certain that it is easy to distinguish between fuel and fresh water. A kettle full of petrol on the stove can make an awful mess. And water in the petrol tank has been known to cause trouble ! Further, when you come to installing the deck equipment, use flush filler caps. On a small boat the type which stands proud is bound to be tripped over in the dark, and may put someone's life in jeopardy. It is often simpler to have the filler direct in the tank and bring a hose into the cabin. A little mopping up after filling is worth it for the simplicity and freedom from more pipes than necessary.

Access to Tanks

The top of each tank will have a circular inspection hole of about 1 ft. in diameter. Make a plywood disc about 2 in. in diameter larger than the hole, drill eight holes evenly spaced and on a circle $\frac{1}{2}$ in. from the main hole's circumference, to take $\frac{1}{4}$ in. alloy or stainless steel cheese-headed bolts $\frac{3}{4}$ in. long. Countersink these into the underside of the tank top, and put them into position before sheathing the top with G.R.P.

Drill corresponding holes in the inspection cover, and sheath that. Lastly, put the tank top into position, ideally while the resin on its underside is still wet, and cover the top side with G.R.P., bringing the glass and resin down to bond on to the sides of the tank. While the resin is still wet, fix a circle of flat section cork gasket on to the top, just inside the circle made by the protruding bolts. The cork can be obtained from a car trimming firm. If the resin has

gone off before this is put into position, it can be fixed with a
contact rubber-based glue. For the water tank, plastic foam can be
used if the cork is difficult to obtain.

The inspection hatch will now drop down on to the bolts. Use
large nylon washers, and then the nuts, tightening well down on to
the cork gasket.

The cover should not be put on to the water tank until some weeks
after it has been made, and it may be as long as a year before the
smell of resin disappears. But once it has cured, the water is quite
safe to drink.

It is as well, though, before the top of the tank goes on, to paint
the inside of the f.w. tank with one of the proprietary marine paints
declared suitable for this purpose. The reason is that quite a lot of
light filters in through the side of a G.R.P. yacht, however thick it
may be—and on a small yacht it is not all that thick. The presence of
light in fresh water will cause algae to grow, which is not very
pleasant in a cup of tea.

Draining Fuel   When installing the fuel tanks, the ideal is to have them in such a
position that they can easily be drained and cleaned out; for dirt and
sludge will inevitably collect at the bottom of the tank. A power boat,
especially when thumping about at speed or in a heavy sea, will
ensure that the sludge gets well churned up—with the inevitable
result that the engine fails just when it is most wanted. The worse
the weather, the more the crew rely on it.

In a small craft such as the type we are dealing with, draining the
tank is bound to be a problem; though with wise installation the
inspection cover will be reasonably easy to get at. In port, that is; not
with the boat heaving about; and anyway, with the carburettor jets
blocked, or the filters, or the injector nozzles, there is no percentage
in cleaning out the tank. Or if there is, no one will feel like doing it.

Header Tank   It is a good idea, when arranging the inside of the boat, to
provide an extra fuel tank, holding only two or three gallons,
positioning it not too near—but higher than—the fuel intake of the
engine. This will be a daily service tank, into which fuel is pumped
for use and from which it is gravity fed to the engine. Filters which
are easily accessible can be provided both sides of this tank, which
itself will be easily accessible.

More details of this type of installation can be obtained from the
book 'High Speed Motor Boats', by John Teale. And this is a book
well worth reading by anyone intending to build a motor yacht, high
speed or not. On this subject of fuel supply, for example, he gives a
lot of very good advice about the types of pump to instal, etc.

The rest of the fitting out will be up to individual owners—the
positioning of bunks, galleys, marine toilet, etc. Don't forget to place
the galley as near amidships as possible, however; and certainly not
up in the bows, if you expect the pots to stay on the stove.

If building deck and coachroof of timber, to be bonded on to the
G.R.P. hull, don't forget, either, that while it may be possible to

provide 6 ft. of headroom in a 20 ft. hull, the outward appearance of
the boat will be pretty dreadful if you do; and the adage that if a
boat looks good she is good, applies equally in reverse. High
topsides for a short length provide too much windage and, sail or
power, make a boat hard to control and, in certain weather
conditions, maybe downright dangerous. Go for beauty, as well as
comfort.

Electrical Before starting on the accommodation, the amateur should sit
down with what drawings he has made and work out a wiring
diagram. It is much too easy to leave all thought of wiring until the
last moment—lights and other electrics are, after all, the gilding on
the lily—better make sure it floats before too much time is wasted on
circuitry.

But this is the wrong attitude. If it is left, one day realization
dawns that the bulkheads, deck head, panelling and so on are neatly
in position; and that either this all has to come down again in order
to instal the wiring, or the cable has to be pinned on the outside,
thus spoiling an otherwise excellent job.

Decide in the beginning, then, what the electricity supply is going
to be—whether accumulator battery of 12 or 24 volts, or, if you are
building that sort of boat, an alternator. If a straight d.c. supply from
a battery, will there be charging equipment, either from the main
engine, or from a separate charging set? Because if so, a switch-
board will be necessary, with a fair amount of wiring involved.

When working out where the interior lights will go, try to position
them so that one light at a time does for most purposes, particularly
if the supply is a battery that has to go ashore for charging. Small
fluorescent lights, now obtainable to work off low voltages, are a
great saving in current. But don't forget that there must be a special,
shaded light for the chart table—or in the area in which the
navigator will be working during night sailing.

A Diagram The best thing is to draw a diagram of the interior and another of
the deck. Mark in where the lights are to go, and at least one power
outlet—you never know when you will become possessed of a
low-voltage dustette. Work out the required circuits—and buy
sufficient cable to make them up. Then, just before panelling,
deckheads, etc. go into place, the cable can be installed section by
section.

This is not the place to go into electrical wiring; there are any
number of books on the subject, and in any case electricians are
always only too eager to talk about their craft. Put your problem to
the man from whom you buy the wire, and the chances are that you
will leave his shop with a complete installation diagram, plus all the
necessary switches, cut-outs, etc. Golden rules are: Use thicker wire
than you would in a domestic circuit. Thin wire sets up too much
resistance for low voltages. Use P.V.C. cable, and solder all
connections. It is essential to keep out damp—which a boat is full of.

Only use electrical equipment purpose-made for marine use, and pay more for it than you can reasonably afford. Re-wiring—which means pulling down all the panelling again—is not something you want to have to do for quite a few years, if at all. Use large switches. Small ones will cause trouble. And when buying interior lights, avoid those which have simple slide-on, slide-off switches. They always give up the ghost in a very short time.

16

Carbon fibre, its use alone or in conjunction with glass. Moulding complete panels for specific purposes. And a method of building a G.R.P. tender.

One of the things we have not yet touched on is the use of carbon fibres. This was hailed a few years ago as the wonder material of the age, and then applied to specific tasks such as turbine blades, which were often too much even for the finest steels. Not unexpectedly, snags developed, and it may be that carbon fibres are not quite so wondrous as they once seemed. Nevertheless, used as a reinforcement for synthetic resin, in place of or in addition to glass fibres, they make a material of surprising strength.

If carbon fibres were as cheap as glass fibres, then there is no doubt that boats, and aeroplanes, and many other things needing high stress cladding, would make use of them. The process of producing carbon fibre is an expensive one, as the natural fibres have to be heated in crucibles instantaneously to very high temperatures.

Tensile Strength
Against a specific gravity for high tensile steel of 7.87, Glass Reinforced Plastics has a factor of 1.7, and so does Carbon Fibre Reinforced Plastics. But against a tensile strength for high tensile steel of 24, for a given weight, the figure for G.R.P. is 70, and that for C.F.R.P. is 120. Figures for stiffness, or resistance to bending (which is perhaps the most important factor when it comes to marine use) are: high tensile steel 3.7, G.R.P. 2.41, C.F.R.P. 20. This makes Carbon Fibre Reinforced Plastics five times stiffer than steel, and eight times stiffer than G.R.P.

What do we, as amateurs, want with this sort of strength? One does not use a piece of fine steel to repair a hole in a matchbox, and neither is there any point in using carbon fibres to repair a hole in a G.R.P. hull. There could, on the other hand, be a lot of point in using it to reinforce sections of a dinghy, and it would be useful, too, when moulding a partition or bulkhead, because the additional strength means that one needs to use less weight of material to obtain the minimum strength required. Carbon fibres are now obtainable from almost any firm which supplies glass and resin. It is supplied in 'tows', which are bunches of the carbon filaments made up into thin ropes. There are 10,000 filaments in each tow, these latter being fluffy and springy, and treated in such a manner that they hold together when wetted out with brush or roller. It is usual to supply the tows in lengths of one metre, singly or in packs, each tow weighing approximately one gramme.

To make full use of the material, and get the strength indicated by the figures given earlier, carbon fibres are used to reinforce polyester resin at a ratio of 60 carbon to 40 resin. To make, say, a samson post capable of holding Q.E. 2, the fibres are laid in a steel mould and the resin poured in on top—making sure, of course, that it permeates the carbon thoroughly. Alternatively, a thin sheet, suitable for a partition, can be made by the hand lay-up method, in exactly the same manner as if using glass rovings. Using carbon fibres in this manner is far too expensive for any possible purpose we might have, for a C.F.R.P. sheet of laminate weighing about a pound will require 300 tows, and this will cost in the region of £60. A far more reasonable way to use the material is to incorporate it into a normal G.R.P. layup.

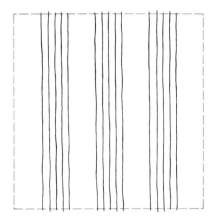

Fig. 47   Carbon fibre in tows, laid out at 3 in. spacing for a 12 in. square surface

Fortunately a good deal of extra strength may be obtained by using 90 per cent of glass fibres to 10 per cent of carbon fibres, by weight. For example, an orthodox glass fibre laminate of two layers of $1\frac{1}{2}$ ounce chopped strand mat may be replaced by a combined laminate using one layer of $1\frac{1}{2}$ ounce chopped strand mat, which weighs 42 grammes per square foot, and 5 grammes of carbon fibre per square foot, the latter in the form of five 1-metre tows (each weighing approximately 1 gramme). The resulting laminate will be about 30 per cent lighter than the corresponding G.R.P. one, and will have equivalent strength.

Directional   Carbon fibre is highly directional in its stiffness and tensile
strength, both being along the line of the filaments, and not at right
angles to it. It is therefore important to make sure in which
direction stiffness is most required, and apply the tows accordingly.
Having decided which way they are to run, lay the tows in bunches
of five in parallel lines at 3 in. spacing (Fig. 47). For each square
foot of laminate, 15 ft. or approximately 5 metres of tow are required.
So a 10-metre pack, costing £2 from a firm such as Trylon, will be
sufficient to reinforce two square feet, and the cost of the carbon
fibre is £1 per square foot. If stiffness and strength are required in
both directions, what is called a 'tartan' lay-up is made, which is
simply running the tows at 3 in. intervals in both directions, i.e. in a
grid (Fig. 48). The same weight of carbon fibre is used per square
foot.

When using carbon fibres, it is even more important than with

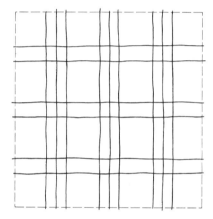

Fig. 48   Carbon fibre laid out in a "tartan" lay up on a 12 in.
square surface

glass rovings that the fibres should be thoroughly soaked with
resin—dry areas will be areas of absolute weakness. Special thin
resins can be bought to make this easier, and it is a good idea to lay
a surface tissue over the tows, especially where they are being used
in grid formation, to keep them in place while wetting out. These thin
resins need an activator as well as a catalyst; each supplier will be
able to advise about his particular material.

Complete   It is very useful to mould complete G.R.P. articles, such as
Articles   flat panels for partitions. On my boat the anchor chain came through

the hawse pipe and piled itself into a small bin forward of the samson post. I carry only 15 fathoms, but as this builds up when getting the anchor in, particularly if the boat is pitching, it often spills over on to the forward bunk cushions. In any case, it is wet and smelly. Accordingly, I decided to close the chain locker off—with G.R.P. because the action of the chain would soon rub the paint off wood, which would then be permanently wet. I therefore measured up the area where I wanted the partition to fit—a tricky shape, with the curved sides of the hull right up in the bows, and an uneven deckhead—then made a stiff brown paper pattern to that size. This was offered up and altered until it fitted. Then a hardboard template was made from the paper pattern, and in turn offered up and trimmed to fit.

I then bought some sheets of a clear plastic purpose-designed for the job—resin won't stick to it. The Strand Glass Co. from which I bought mine, call theirs Melinex, but other firms may have different names. This was cut to cover the hardboard. I put a layer of gel coat, coloured with pigment, over the Melinex, then layed-up chopped strand mat and resin to the thickness of $\frac{1}{8}$ in. On top of this I put another sheet of Melinex, and left it to cure. When ready I trimmed the edges down to the hardboard panel's size, put the G.R.P. panel into position and bonded it in with glass tape and resin. As ventilation in the chain locker was obviously necessary, I drilled some $\frac{1}{2}$ in. holes in the panel and put a metal ventilator over them. At a later date I also found that an inspection panel was necessary, and cut one 6 in. square—large enough to get an arm in—and closed it with a 7 in. square of marine ply fastened with a hardwood dog on each of the four sides (Fig. 49). Had I thought of this earlier I should, of course, have put a 6 in. square of wood on to the hardboard template, and 'moulded the hole in'.

I did not use carbon fibres in this panel, because I did not think that it needed that much strength, and it did not justify the expense. It would have been easy enough to put the 'tartan' pattern in, however. This book has nothing to do with boatbuilding, as such, but without going into any of the technicalities of design and framing, I can pass on a tip which makes moulding a G.R.P. tender easier than building in plywood. There is no shortage of designs; a dozen or more books in any public library will give the outlines of the particular author's idea of what a good tender should be like—nearly always plywood built. Or anyone who has ever used a small dinghy for this purpose will have his own opinion.

According to how big the parent yacht is, and assuming it is desired to have a solid dinghy as tender on deck or to tow, it will be 7 ft. long or more, with a good beam, either pram or stem according to preference, with a rise towards the bows, flat sections aft, and with a reasonable skeg to help directional stability when rowing and towing. Having decided on the dimensions, the builder starts off as though working in plywood, putting down the keel, transom, bow, gunwale and chines, and one or more temporary building frames according to the size of the boat. Working, of course, with this frame

upside down, the whole is then covered with muslin, cutting the
material out in panels to fit each section, tacking it down and
pulling it as tight as possible.

This is then sprayed with something which is wet to begin with,
but which dries hard, and is inert, such as aerosol starch. The liquid

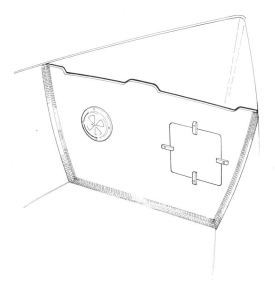

Fig. 49   G.R.P. panel in bows with ventilator and inspection hatch

shrinks the muslin, pulling it tight and forcing concave curves where
the pull is in two directions, particularly between gunwale and chine
in the bow section. When the starch hardens, the curves remain.

The wooden frames and the muslin will remain as an integral part
of the boat, so there is no release agent required. Merely lay resin and
glass on top of what is effectively a male mould, laminating until a
sufficient thickness is built up—and don't forget that weight can be
saved if some carbon fibres are included, perhaps just in the
underwater sections, where a tender takes most knocks. A layer of
pigmented gel coat is put on finally, and when this is cured any
temporary frames are cut out and the hull completed with bonded-in
thwarts, etc. The outside of the hull will not have the beautiful
regularity which a professionally made hull from a female mould has.
But it will be a lot less expensive; and in fact as good a finish as one
is willing to work for can be obtained. It just needs lots of elbow
grease and reams of wet and dry paper.

One of the selling points of the G.R.P. yacht is that it needs little maintenance. And this is a just claim, not just a selling gimmick, as I have already proved. Theoretically, at the end of a season's sailing, the vessel can be put into a mud berth or into a cradle in a field, and forgotten about until next Spring. Again, this is more than theory. G.R.P. does not deteriorate in fact but, if the owner wants to keep his boat smart, certain things should be done at laying up time—not the time-consuming essential tasks as for the wooden boat; but enough jobs to keep him moderately busy for a weekend or two.

In the first place, the boat should have an adequate cover, which is large enough to go over a trestle spanning the length of the deck from bows to stern. It should cover the deck completely and fall well down the sides of the hull. It should, if possible, be of good heavy rot-proof canvas. A tarpaulin cover large enough for a 21 ft. yacht will probably cost between £30 and £40; but if looked after it will well outlast the life of the boat; and of course it is an asset when the owner comes to sell. The cost of the cover, in any case, is only a fraction of the value of the yacht, and it is important as an aid to retaining that value. There are cheaper types of tarpaulin 'recommended' for boat covers, but not by me. Certainly not polythene, nor rubberized sheeting. For although the boat should be protected, it is essential to allow air to circulate over and around it freely; in spite of the fact that it is made of rot-proof plastics, there is still a good deal of wood on board. There is also, no doubt, some fabric though everything possible should be removed; and both wood and fabric will attract the spores of mildew unless there is ample ventilation.

Canvas tarpaulin is both waterproof and porous. Plastic and rubber is not. The trestle is essential for the same reason—to hold the top of the tarpaulin away from the deck, allowing air to circulate. It must be left open at each end, in an inverted 'V'—and it is ideal, too, to leave both fore and aft hatches open, or ajar, so that the draught can circulate below. But this will depend very much on where the boat is laid up. It is not possible to leave hatches open in a district where security is a problem or vandals might get aboard.

As G.R.P. is such a marvellous material, you may say, what reason is there for covering it at all ? By leaving the hull exposed, no ventilation problems are experienced.

Danger from Ice Unfortunately, besides a slight discolouration from weathering—in some colours, anyway—G.R.P. can suffer from another disfigurement during winter lay up. No matter how carefully the yacht has been treated, the gel coat is bound to have suffered, even if only by microscopic cracks, cuts and scratches, during a sailing season. If water gets into these, and lies, a sharp spell of frost will freeze it. With the result that the natural expansion of water into ice will break off larger pieces of the plastic.

These are not likely to impair the efficiency of the hull. But they will make it shabby, and the whole expanse will have to be filled and painted much earlier than would otherwise have been the case.

There is, too, the fact that woodwork on deck—locker lids and doors in the cockpit, grab rails, washboards, the sliding hatch—will lose their varnish very quickly in winter weather if not protected. And once the varnish has gone, the wood—mahogany particularly— soon discolours. When the new coats of varnish are applied, that discoloration will come up as a dark grey, showing badly against the rich red of the normal woodwork. If, in spite of everything, the wood becomes discoloured, I recommend a preparation called 'Colorbak', which can be bought in most marine chandlery stores. It is brushed on to the wood, left for a while according to the instructions, then washed off. When dry, varnish is put on in the normal way. When putting on the varnish, don't be disappointed, as I was, that the wood still seems grey after using this preparation. In my case, anyway, by the time the varnish has dried the mahogany colour was in full bloom again.

The right time to apply paint and varnish is as soon as the boat comes out of the water. Few people are strong minded enough for this, but reasons for doing it in the autumn are first, that the varnish helps protect the woodwork ; and second, if the hull has already been painted once it is wise to put another coat on within twelve months. After that period, the first coat is likely to have become so brittle that it will be difficult to key the new coat to it. Moreover, it may chip underneath the new coat at the slightest knock. If it is not being painted for next season, and is still the bare G.R.P., give the hull a good coating of wax polish—one of those specially made for fibre glass.

Even if time, or laziness, preclude an owner from doing the things which need doing to protect his glass fibre yacht and keep it looking beautiful, he must not forget all the jobs which are just as essential with G.R.P. as they are with wood or steel.

Briefly, the main jobs to be done are :

(a) Take the sails home and clean them. Terylene and other synthetic fibre sails normally only need sponging over with warm water in which a little mild detergent such as washing up liquid is mixed. Some people recommend putting them in the washing machine, but this involves taking all the metal fittings off, and I don't recommend it.

Care of Sails   Don't use chemicals to get out stains; if they won't come out with water and detergent, leave them alone. When the sails are as clean as possible, hang them up to dry thoroughly—synthetic fibres won't rot if put away wet, but they will grow mildew spots. Examine piston and spring hanks and give each moving part just a tiny smear of stain proof lubricant which can be obtained from sailmakers. Examine all sewn fastenings, and any which look frayed or doubtful should be cut out and sewn again, using Terylene or nylon thread.

Also examine, inch by inch, all the seams. Because synthetic thread does not bed down well into synthetic sail cloth, the seams are always proud, and sooner or later fray. If these can be repaired at home, get it done immediately. Don't put off until Spring what can be done now, in fact, for it may then easily get overlooked until, in a blow next season, the whole seam tears out. If a major sail repair is needed, or new sails required, go along to the sailmaker immediately. He needs work during the winter, and will probably offer a discount to get it. If the order is not placed until Spring, the customer is likely to be at the end of a queue which will keep him waiting until next autumn.

(b) Remove all bunk cushions and mattresses, curtains, etc., take them home, clean where necessary, and store in a warm dry place.

(c) Empty fuel and water tanks, and leave the tops open, but protected with muslin or something similar, so that air but not dirt can get in.

(d) Empty food lockers and clean them thoroughly with hot water, detergent and disinfectant.

(e) Open and leave open all locker doors, traps in the cabin sole, etc.

In my own G.R.P. yacht there at one time always seemed to be a musty smell. Because it is a bilge keel boat, the space between the cabin sole and the bottom is only about 1 in., with only one 6 in. square trap giving access to it. Consequently this space could never be adequately cleaned.

Then I was given a plastic bag full of some granulated material which was advertized as being to stop mildew in the bilges of wooden boats. It had to be placed in the bilge as it was, still inside the plastic bag. I stuffed it with difficulty into the tiny space between cabin sole and hull, and ever since have enjoyed a faint antiseptic odour throughout the cabin—a welcome change to the previous one of mildew.

(f) Pump out the marine toilet with fresh water, then water and disinfectant, and then a pint of paraffin. The last flush will prevent washers getting sticky and jamming. Finally read the instructions for the particular make of toilet, and carry out religiously whatever they say. Some makes have a plug in the base, situated so that it would never be thought of unless the instructions called it to mind. This has to be opened to remove the last traces of water from the system— water which, if left, may freeze and cause serious damage.

(g) Take all easily removable navigational and other equipment ashore, carefully protected. That is, compasses (steering and hand) ; logs, echo sounding equipment, clocks, barometers. Leaving them on board is not only subjecting them unnecessarily to the winter's damp, but a temptation to any potential thief who may look through the portholes to see whether the yacht is worth breaking into.

(h) Remove the rigging, examine standing and running gear and discard any which is frayed. Grease sheaves and blocks. Rub vaseline into stainless or galvanized wire, grease bottle screws, etc., and label each shroud and halliard so that no confusion arises in the Spring when it all goes together again.

Examine the mast and boom for deterioration. A wooden mast might have a patch of rot, or be split, and this can be repaired professionally in most cases. An aluminium or steel mast may crack, or come apart at a seam, and this will require expert attention too. It will probably have to be sent away for welding. Mast fittings should be examined at the same time, and replaced if there is any sign of metal fatigue or actual fracture. Spars should be stored under cover during the winter, not left in the open.

The winter is the time to get on with all the improvements which we have discussed in the previous pages, and the many others which will be sparked off just by giving thought to possibilities. The main thing about fibre glass is to treat it for what it is. Not to be wishing all the time that it was wood, or in some way more 'boat-like'.

Remember that the first men would have been glad to have found a G.R.P. hull already made, instead of having to go to all the trouble of hollowing out a tree trunk. Wood, in its time, has been all right as far as it went. G.R.P. is better, for it has none of the faults of wood, certainly from the viewpoint of yacht maintenance. So make the most of G.R.P. You are extremely fortunate to have it.